921 BAI
The Tour

MW01351219

DATE DUE

THE LIBRARY STORE #47-0206

The Tour

Copyright © 2009 Larry Bain

No part of this book may be reproduced by any mechanical, photographic, or electronic process, nor may it be otherwise copied for public or private use without prior written permission from the author.

DEDICATION

To my kids Denise, Ryan, and Mathew, for you this is written so you may know what I was like as a kid, and what influences formed me. To my wife, Beverly, who has put up with me the last 40 years, and stuck with me through thick and thin. And to all the men and women who served in the Vietnam war and gave their all. Some, never seeing their families again; and those who made it back, putting up with being shunned by society.

To those men in the field whose sacrifices we will never know, I apologize for not being a better soldier.

ACKNOWLEDGEMENTS

I would like to thank my friends Gene & Linda Thomas for getting the ball rolling. Also thanks to Tracee Curfman whose hard work and diligence put together a beautiful hardcover first edition that I will always cherish. To my sister Carole who took my initial chicken-scratch and put it in a format for me to edit. To my friend and author Charity Maness for her expertise and help in publishing and marketing. And last but not least, thanks to my friend, Jack Forkner, for his hours and hours putting this new edition into a flowing work of which I am proud. His hard work put the book in a format that could be sent to the publisher.

I would also like to thank my nephew, Rick Pisio, for his helicopter pictures; and Ernie Camacho for his pictures of Dak To.

PREFACE

This book documents some of my life experiences, so that in the future you may be able to draw on what you have read. My hope is that it may help you to laugh at what you are experiencing. Before I get into my military experiences, I'll give you some background on how I got to be a citified country bumpkin.

The author, 1968

The Tour

Chapter 1: *pg 9*: In the beginning

Chapter 2: *pg 13:* California here I come

Chapter 3: pg 17: High School Days

Chapter 4: *pg 21*: Property of the US Government

Chapter 5: pg 25: Basic Training

Chapter 6: *pg 31*: More training

Chapter 7: *pg 35*: Winds of Change; The Attack

Chapter 8: *pg 39*: The Big Green Pond

Chapter 9: *pg 41*: Pre-Camo; Overboard

Chapter 10: *pg 45*: The War; Borrow a bullet

Chapter 11: *pg 49*: The Handgun Decision; Our Base for a Year; Doing our job; Preparedness Check ...again; The Coast; The Natives; The Lawn

Chapter 12: *pg 59*: The Coke Attack; The Attitude Adjustment

Chapter 13: *pg 65*: The Mail; The Oasis; The Monsoons; Three Tango

Chapter 14: *pg 71*: Back at Camp; The Oscar; George; Snoopy

Chapter 15: *pg 75*: Being a Crew Chief; Re-up; Duds; Charge of Quarters

Chapter 16: *pg 81*: Volunteering for R&R; Cutting the LZ; Pie in the Sky; Pilots

Chapter 17: *pg 85*: Misery; Pit Stop; Night Life; On the Rebound; New Barracks; Bathroom Lights; One Shot; Agent Orange; Captain Go-Go; Cease Fire; Too Much Dust; New Guy; What's This Button For; Don't Shoot; Love and War; The Race; Hot Pursuit; Smoke; Wild Things

Chapter 18: *pg 101*: The New 'H' Model; Bullets flying; Night Duty; POW; Good-bye Rocks; Bob Hope; Faux Pas; The Deception; Weekend Away; Hill 875; Mortars; Leopard Skin Leotards; Mortars Galore;

Chapter 19: *pg 117*: Going home; Home at Last

Chapter 20: *pg 123*: Fort Knox

Postscript: *pg. 127*

Statistics: *pg. 129*

Links*: pg. 130*

CHAPTER

1

In the beginning...

I was born in New Westminster, British Columbia (near Vancouver) on March 20, 1947. The folks lived on a small farm in the Fraser River valley. The small town had a population of around 200. It was called Websters Corners. If that's not bumpkin enough for you, I don't know what is. Wait it gets better! While we lived there, my Dad tried to make his fortune raising (of all things) chickens. What he did manage to get out of that experience was an extreme dislike of chicken. The area was very rural and my brother Jim tells us that he had to fight off the wolves just to go to the outhouse. Of course, he liked to fight anyway.

We lived there until I was about six, then we moved the 35 miles to Burnaby. It is a suburb of Vancouver. We moved into a brand new house that had a great view of Burrard Inlet, the Second Narrows Bridge, and the Lions Gate Bridge. Across the inlet from us was Grouse Mountain. That was the local ski resort. In the summers I still liked to go out to my Uncle Bert's and Aunt Daisy's farm right beside our old farm.

When I got a little older, there was a garden to help with, hay to be cut and raked; and then with a pitchfork, thrown into a pile. My cousin Richard and I would then have to throw the piles of hay onto a wagon, and Uncle Bert would then take it to the barn. Of course we would get quite an appetite from that hard work; but we had Aunt Daisy's fresh baked bread and garden-fresh vegetables to look forward to. Not to mention the homemade jams and fresh baked pies. In the early years there was a cow that had to be milked — the fresh milk and cream were great. If we didn't have those chores to do, we would head to one of the local creeks to go fishing or exploring or just sit and listen to the water running. I used to love to run through the forest just for the joy of running. It's a wonder some bear or mountain lion didn't get us back then. We never even gave that a thought.

If we had been working particularly hard, Uncle Bert would load us all into the Buick and head for one of the local swimming holes. We always had fun since we loved the water and the break from chores. It was a great life for a kid, and I wouldn't trade those memories for anything.

Back in the city, we had to start being more citified by wearing shoes and clothes and stuff. I was not real happy with the change. Like the boy said, *"I don't want to go to no school where they spell tater with a P."* In order to help with the frustration factor, I started riding my new 3-speed bike.

A school friend and I started off riding to Stanley Park. It was about 10 miles to the park. Once there, we rode around the park to check out all the sites; then we rode home. All in all, we would cover about 23 miles. We were 10 years old. Every Sunday we would go for a ride to some new location.

One Sunday we went across the Second Narrows Bridge and up Grouse Mountain. As we got close to the top, it started getting dark; so we began heading back down. As the cars were bumper-to-bumper going down the mountain, we were often forced to ride off the side of the pavement. We were traveling a lot faster than the cars, and the road was quite steep. The bikes seemed to want to fly down that hill. At one point I was traveling a little too fast, got to close, and hit a car mirror causing me to lose control and go down in the gravel. I slid for a distance before coming to a stop. The people whose car I hit jumped out to see if I was okay. I got up, dusted myself off, said I was okay, and headed on down the hill. We finally made it home, and I was late for dinner; but the folks didn't get upset. Of course they didn't know where I'd been either.

They did get upset, however, when my friend and I rode out to Uncle Bert's and arrived there at 4:00pm one Sunday afternoon. It was 35 miles out there, and I intended on turning around and heading back after a short rest. That was not to happen as Aunt Daisy called the folks and asked "*Do you know where your son is?*" After she informed them, the lid came off the skillet. Uncle Bert had to take a day off work to bring us back to the city, and that made my Dad madder than anything. Of course we missed a day of school, which also made him mad. That was about the end of the riding on Sundays — something about pushing things to the limit. I was still 10 years old when this took place.

Dad worked heavy construction since getting out of the chicken business. He started building dams, pipelines, and fish ladders. Work on the fish ladders in Quesnel, B.C. kept him away from home for long periods of time. This gave my Mom the responsibility of keeping the household in order. She also worked as a nurse during that time. I have the utmost respect for her, as I never heard her complain about the two jobs that she was charged with, and she always seemed in good spirits. It must have been extremely tiring. Work was getting hard to find for Dad, and he was ready for a change. That change turned out to be moving to another country, the USA; and California, he was told, was the land of opportunity.

The Tour

CHAPTER

2

California, here I come…

In June of 1958 we moved to the Bay Area of California. The day we left, the Second Narrows Bridge collapsed. There were 19 people who died in that incident. It loomed as an omen to me. I did not like this move as it made it extremely hard to ride my bike out to Uncle Bert's and Aunt Daisie's. Dad also said I was going to have to learn a new language. I was going to have to say "you all" before or after every sentence.

This area of California was nothing like the area of B.C. that I just came from. There were no forests, no streams, no snow capped mountains, and no snow in the winter. To a kid, those were things that made life fun and interesting. My first summer in California was awful; and I knew if I had a way to go back to B.C., I'd be gone. The great thing about kids though is that they have a way to adapt too many different situations. I was no different. Once we moved into a permanent house in San Leandro, there were kids my age to play ball with, to play roller derby with, and generally just have fun with. Living close to a school with a large playground where we could play football and baseball helped a lot. There were also basketball courts that we could play on in the winter months. After the first couple of years there, I entered John Muir Junior High School. One day after school the track coach had asked me to stay and try running the 1330-yard run (3/4 mile). He had me run against his fastest guy. I didn't know that at the time, but I beat him by about 20 yards. This got the coach buzzing, and he wanted me to run it again in a few days. The only training I had received was what I got in PE class. I did have running in my blood, as my dad was the national champion of Canada in the mile and half mile in his high school years. My brother Jerry ran a 4:20-minute mile in high school, which earned him a scholarship to the University of Washington the following year. A few days later, I ran the 3/4-mile again. This time I was running against the clock, with three different guys each running a quarter mile. Apparently I beat Owen Hoffman's record at that school. (Owen was a track star at Pacific High who later went on to the state meet running the 1/2-mile.) Owen, however, had dedication. He used to run to school carrying his books, have track practice after school, and then run home. I was lucky if I could walk after practice, never even thinking of running the 3-1/2 miles home. Once home, I would collapse on the couch and go to sleep.

I developed other interests that kept me occupied. I soon was able to take a scuba diving course that was offered through the Red Cross. It was held at Arroyo High School, and included a number of mandatory ocean dives. It was a tough course, and I was the youngest one there. I passed the course, and I certainly need to thank my parents for taking me to all the ocean dives. And so it was at 14 years old, I became a scuba diver.

When school got out for the summer, I got on a bus and went back to British Columbia to spend the summer at Uncle Bert's and Aunt Daisie's. Cousin Richard and I got a job working on a farm stacking bales of hay on a wagon that followed behind a baler. It was tough work for young kids, but we didn't mind. The worst part was the thirst we would get. We were offered one of two things to drink. The first being 7UP. That, we discovered, only made us thirstier. The second thing offered was beer. This was a taste that had to be acquired. There really wasn't time to just sip the stuff so we learned to just belt it down. By the time we got home late in the evening, we really were a sight! We were working 12 to 16-hours a day. So for several summers I would get on a bus, go back to B.C., and work on the farm for the summer. Come September, I'd go back to California.

The Tour

CHAPTER

3

High school days...

September always brought cross-country season. Most courses were about 2-1/2 miles, and included a number of hills to get up. Trying to get into shape after not running all summer was always difficult. I don't know if I ever was in shape. In the spring of my junior year we had a track meet against Fremont High School of Oakland. I was to run the mile. The problem was that they did not have a 1/4-mile track. It was a dirt playground that they marked out an oval. The mile run consisted of running 7 or 8 times around this oval. Once the race was on, and I had gone around about 5 times; I lost count. I had no idea how many more laps were left, so I kept on running like it was my last one. I did manage to finish the race and actually won. It was the fastest time I ever had in the mile—4min. 30 sec. For a junior that wasn't too bad.

One great life lesson I learned at that track meet was during the high hurdle event. That event was supposed to be 120 yards, but there wasn't a stretch that long. So this event was 100-yard high hurdles. This school had some excellent sprint men; and Leroy was no exception. As the race neared the halfway point, he was in the lead. As he passed in front of the stands, he tripped over a hurdle and fell to the ground. His friends in the stands laughed at him and taunted him. He stood up, looked at his friends in the stands, turned around and took off running. He won that race.

Running took a lot out of me, and I decided that my senior year I needed to keep my grades up if I wanted to go to college. So I did not compete in track my senior year. I did, however, get a car, and that required that I get a job to pay for insurance, gas, and maintenance. Not to mention spending money. I got a job washing dishes at a restaurant in San Lorenzo. This job would get me through until the summer when I would once again head for B.C. to spend the summer working. This time was different; my sister Carole wanted to go with me.

We drove my 1958 Ford Skyliner, and drove straight through. Twenty-three hours of driving was a long time to be sitting; and when we arrived at Uncle Bert's, I could sure feel the effects. It turns out that our job on the farm was no longer there, but I don't remember why.

Jack, a long time friend of Cousin Richard and mine, suggested we go up to where his brother was working—the Prince George area of northern B.C. We arrived at a place on Francois Lake; a very beautiful place that one might say was a little primitive. They did not have power, but the most significant thing was they still had crank phones. Two longs and a short was the neighbors, one long and two shorts was yours, etc. We spent two days in the area, and the final result was there was no work for us. It didn't help that there were three of us looking for work. I think Jack could have stayed and found work, but he probably felt bad that he got us to drive all the way there and not find work.

Back on the road we headed back to Prince George. There we started asking around, and eventually found work with the railroad. It was hot in the area and we got to sleep in old wooden railroad cars. They were hotter than the temperature outside, which was hovering around 95°. Considering that it didn't get dark until 11:00pm, sleep was hard to get. Most days were spent carrying creosoted railroad ties. They were heavy; and by the end of the day my arms would cramp up, and I would suffer when it was shower time. The people that were a part of this crew left me with the feeling that we needed to watch our backs. Most were immigrants trying to make it in a new country. They were a rough bunch that I never felt comfortable around. After a couple weeks of that, I was ready to move on. This was not something that had a future. Cousin Richard stayed; Jack and I moved on.

Richard eventually got a decent job as the water boy. Jack and I headed back to California. The one thing of note with that trip was when we got to the mountains in southern Oregon, the transmission on the car refused to go any more. We pulled over and slept for the night. In the morning when things were cooler, it made it up the rest of the way to the top, and down the other side. Part way back in northern California, we had to stop and get some 90-weight oil to put in the transmission. That allowed us to get back to San Leandro.

We both looked for work, and it wasn't long before Jack got discouraged and decided to take the bus back to B.C. A few days after he left, Carole called and told me about a job at a cabinet shop in Castro Valley. I talked to the owner, Larry, and he gave me the job. So after driving over 3000 miles, I get a job about 10 miles from our house. It was for minimum wage, but it was a start. After my military service, I was able to start an apprenticeship with him. For the time being, I was able to work the summer for him and I started at Chabot College in the fall. I was deferred from the draft while attending college, but this was not to last long. After a couple of months, the Selective Service Board reclassified me to 1A—available immediately for military service. The Vietnam war was cranking up, and they wanted people to send there. At that point in time, if you were reclassified, you had about 30 days to take care of business before you were drafted. I did not want to end up in the infantry walking the jungle. So, I enlisted as a helicopter mechanic.

The Tour

CHAPTER

4

Property of the U.S. Government...

Induction into the Army occurred in Oakland, California November 22, 1965. At 18 years old and being a somewhat innocent youth, the reality of the situation came crashing-in all too sudden. Even though I had left home for the summer many times before, this was totally different. I could not get over the feeling that we had all become pawns in a very serious game. The feeling I got from now being just a number, with no one giving a damn what you think or feel, was something I would never get used to. At the airport, waiting to be shipped off to basic training, I met a young guy (although older than myself) whose friendship I cherish to this day. Marty, an ex- college football player, had a confidence that I did not have at the time. He was on his way to Fort Polk, as was I. We were placed in the same company for basic training; and as it turned out, followed each other most of the way through our Army days.

Many of the men inducted that day were sent to different places for basic training. Most soldiers inducted in California were sent to Fort Ord in California. Marty and I were sent to Fort Polk, Louisiana. After a flight that ended at Lake Charles, Louisiana and a bus ride to the base, we were greeted with a lot of yelling and carrying on about family heritage and stuff having to do with not really being men. In fact, I'm pretty sure they referred to us as little creatures that crawled around on rotting meat. On the 23rd of November it was stifling. The humidity was something I was not used to. The base seemed to be out in the middle of nowhere. There seemed to be no hills or valleys, just flat ground with pine trees everywhere.

Getting off the bus on that day ushered in a whole new and unknown way life. We were not people; we were now **Property of the U.S. Government**. Although I believe a drill sergeant later had claimed part of us as his own, stating in a Philippine accent, "Your heart and soul may belong to God, but your ass belongs to me." I immediately saw the conflict he was in, but figured he would have to work that out. Being the new guy and trying to offer a correction was probably not the wisest thing at this time. Fighting the urge to open my mouth was the battle I had to fight.

So we were herded like cattle through processing, where we were given a nifty haircut and clothing, along with a duffle bag to hold it all. There were no tie dyed "T" shirts, no bell-bottomed pants, no "make love, not war" stickers for our belongings. These guys were serious. However, these were the sixties, wasn't it time to update? Perhaps if someone just dropped a little suggestion.

Next, if I were naming colors, olive drab, would not be a color; it is a statement. It is a philosophy, and for many, a way of life. I think because everything was this *color*, there must have been a shortage of *color coordinators* or a complete lack of imagination. That's the only logical conclusion I could draw. But then, I was from California. This was not a place that people from other parts of the country looked up to. The joke being, "Do you know how they separate the men from the boys in California?" The answer: "With a crow bar!"

Our days began at 3:30am with the wake-up call. Sergeants coming in and yelling to get up, get dressed, and "fall out", which meant get in line. Platoons were organized, and leaders were picked. At 4:30am every morning, we would go on a mile run. After the run, we would line up at the mess hall for breakfast. Once we made it through the door, we were given 3 minutes to eat. Of course, drill sergeants were in the mess hall to make sure no one took 4 minutes.

    Training continued; teaching us how to march and learning our right from our left. At the outset, that doesn't seem like a difficult thing to master. But with 30 guys wondering at this point why the hell they joined the Army, no one was thinking about their feet. Only one guy needed to screw up at any given moment, and we all ended up with our left pocket full of rocks. I did not realize that 5 pounds of rock would fit in the left front pocket of military fatigues. I know now! So we marched with a pocket full of rocks, on and on. Having grown up in the country in the early part of my life, and having thrown rocks as a sport and a means of self-defense; it did not escape me that we had not yet been issued weapons. Was this a new battle plan? Maybe! I did not see it as a confidence builder. As the weeks went on, we were taught hand-to-hand combat, to throw grenades, concealment, and even firing an M-14 rifle.

The Tour

CHAPTER

5

Basic Training...

The day would come when we had to go out on a bivouac (camping). We had a backpack with a change of clothes, miscellaneous toiletries, extra boots, etc. The pack probably weighed 30 pounds. The M-14 rifle weighed about 12 pounds. For several days we ran here and there for this training or that. Then one night we had to break camp at about 1:00am. We put on our packs, slung our rifles and 60-pound duffle bag over our shoulders, and ran double-time for 2 miles. This did not work out well for me. When the duffle bag was on my shoulder, I could not breathe well. Having to run double-time created more of a need for air, so something had to give. I made it the 2 miles; but when I got there, both my legs were cramped solid. Every muscle in both legs was tuned to High C. The pain was the worst I have ever experienced. My mind had the cure. As I was standing in formation - swaying as if drunk - a sergeant decided to make me stand still. He started smacking me around. I felt nothing. What happened next I cannot explain; nor do I know the full implications. Apparently I passed out. But while in that state, part of me left the body on the ground and hovered about 15 feet above. I could see nothing, but I could hear what they were saying and felt a total peace. I wonder if I had known the Lord then, if I could have seen or even talked to Him. But there was nothing but total darkness. I don't know how long this went on, but I think it was for some time. When I returned to my earthly body, I was in the back seat of a jeep and two guys were taking me to a hospital. The first thing I noticed was that my fingers were terribly distorted. I yelled to the guys in front to look at how distorted my fingers were, and got *the look*. You know the one. At the time, I did not care; but they must have thought, boy, this guy is out there. Of course, it was just my vision that was distorted.

When we arrived at the base hospital, one of the first things was to have a bath since I had been lying in mud. That taken care of, I discovered I could not walk. Try as I might, my legs would not hold me up. My days of running track flashed through my mind. Would I no longer be able to run or walk? The next order of business was a urine sample. The urine was the color of black coffee. That was scary. The nurses questioned me about what I put in it, and gave me another of *the looks*. This just wasn't my day; and it was about to get worse.

As I was taken back to my bed, a lieutenant appeared and asked if I was Pvt. Bain. I answered, "Yes" and he said, "Sorry to inform you, but your brother is dead." The numbing effect of my condition softened the blow somewhat, but my question to him was, "Which brother?" He did not know. He suggested I call home and find out. This was his big mistake. Upon calling home, waking my mom at 3:00am, and asking her a question like that meant the fury was about to be unleashed. She knew nothing about either of her other sons being killed. But that got her checking. It turns out that it was a mistake. Unfortunately a *McBain* had lost his brother. This I did not find out until weeks later. My mother, in the meantime, had called and written to the Company Commander to let him know that she did not appreciate the scare she had received and what kind of company was he running? When I did return to the company, this translated into me being called in front of the Company Commander to receive an apology of sorts.

So, while in the hospital I came down with pneumonia. I had 103°-104° temperature, which meant they had to put me in a bathtub full of ice water. It's a good thing my heart had been strong; because if anything tests it to its limits, it would be that dunk in the tub. My friend Marty also came down with pneumonia, and was in the hospital at the same time.

For 3 weeks, I fought that pneumonia and was unable to walk. Finally they told me I would have to leave the hospital or be recycled (start my training over). I had to take another series of tests, so they had me push another fellow in a wheel chair to another building for testing. Not being able to walk for 3 weeks, and being told to push someone else down a series of ramps, was a challenge I didn't think I was up to. We made it, with me holding myself up with the wheel chair. The trip back, however, was not so easy. Pushing the wheel chair up the ramps was not something my legs were prepared for. I made it halfway up the last ramp of our building, and my legs gave out. I was able to stop the wheel chair from running me over, but how was I going to get it up the ramp. Obviously, no one was around to help. Finally, I maneuvered around to where my back was against the wheel chair with my butt on the ramp and my legs out. I brought my knees up towards my chest with my feet and hands on the deck and pushed. Six inches at a time we progressed up the ramp. Finally we were on the flat part, and I was able to get up without the wheelchair taking off. We finished our journey and within an hour, I was on my way back to my unit. Upon arriving there, all the troops were out training; so being exhausted, I decided to take a nap. Wrong! I woke up to see my drill sergeant, with his face inches away from mine yelling, "What are you doing soldier?" That little nap gave me a free ticket to latrine duty. Shining all the brass with *Brasso* and a toothbrush really makes you appreciate the beauty of those appliances. I was up late shining those things.

The Tour

The next morning started as usual at 3:30am with calisthenics and the mile run. How I was able to run that mile, I do not know. I believe God was with me again. Having made it through that, the rest of my training got easier as time went on.

One of the things that sticks out in my mind, was the drill sergeant telling us to go do some physical exercise, then immediately yelling at us, "Quickly, quickly, you should have been back here already." That was very typical of the type of pressure used to motivate the troops on a daily basis. The final test was a 1-mile run for time. I worried about that run. Would my legs hold up? Would I fade really badly at the end? I felt I had something to prove at that point, and I wanted to do well. I believe I ran one of the fastest times—in combat boots.

My basic training was complete, and we had a graduation and parade in front of military dignitaries. We were allowed to take the rocks out of our pockets finally, so the marching was easier than normal. After the graduation, we were given a 30-day leave to go home. Marty and I were booked on a flight on Trans Texas Airlines along with 150 other soldiers to go from Lake Charles, Louisiana to Dallas, Texas on a DC-3. The old prop driven plane would hold about 30 passengers, so someone was going to have to wait for a later aircraft. Thankfully, it wasn't us. As we

flew towards Dallas, I noticed the right engine was leaking oil from the front of the wing. I couldn't see the left wing. I also noticed that the plane was flying low level for the majority of the trip. As I watched the wings flap in the wind, I thought they just

weren't flapping hard enough to gain the altitude that it should have. But it sure was trying.

The Tour

CHAPTER

6

More training...

My military testing was not over though. Within 30 days of passing out, I came down with Bells Palsy. The left side of my face was paralyzed. This meant that I could not blink my left eye. The Army gave me an eye patch to wear and some glycerin to lubricate the eye. The result of that affliction still affects me today. In some people it goes away in weeks; others months. For me, my eye waters whenever it wants, giving me blurry vision until I wipe it.

After our leave, Marty and I were sent for advanced training at Fort Rucker, Alabama. This was helicopter mechanic school for me. I got to wear an eye patch that a friend had drawn an eyeball on. Now I was normal. Marty had signed up for fixed wing aircraft maintenance, so our classes soon became different. Helicopter schooling was done in a World War II base that consisted mostly of wooden buildings. We were placed in an area of wooden buildings resurrected from the 1940's. It was hot in Alabama in the spring of 1966. One of the things done for fun by some of the guys in their off time was to go looking for snakes. Snakes they found. One rattlesnake was about 3½ feet long and was about 3 to 4 inches in diameter. They cut the head off and pinned the snake up to the bulletin board. Someone also caught a coral snake and did the same to that one. As I said, this area had not been occupied since WW II. Helicopter training was geared towards preparing us for our inevitable

The Tour

trip to Vietnam. Many of the instructors, having just come back, were more than willing to tell us their stories of survival and war.

After 3 months of helicopter training, we were given our next assignment. I was sent to Fort Lewis, Washington; Marty stayed for additional training. This assignment was to a holding company where we were assigned different tasks. I was assigned to work in a film library that was organized and run by civilian employees. It was a sometimes-interesting job, and I took every opportunity to watch the latest films on Vietnam—trying to see what I was in for.

I enjoyed my time at Ft. Lewis; taking every opportunity to workout with weights, run on the ¼ mile track, and use the sauna. Marty arrived at Ft. Lewis a month or so later, and we got caught up on the latest news. There were many new friends that had been made in schooling that made the Army experience much more enjoyable.

One of these friends was a guy named George. He had a private pilot's license and loved to fly. He joined the flying club on the base, and was soon flying all over the area. In the summer of 1966, George and I flew a Piper Tri-pacer to the Abbotsford Air Show in Canada. It was a high wing aircraft that was very slow. Part way up to the show, George got tired and wanted to rest. He found an abandoned runway and proceeded to land there. Once on the ground we discovered that we were in a bit of a predicament. The runway on which we landed was extremely short with a tall bunch of trees at the end. It looked doubtful that we could get the airspeed needed to get out of this place. The airstrip seemed to be out in the middle of nowhere with no buildings or signs of human habitation anywhere. We finally just decided to go for it. If we didn't make it we would crash and probably be killed. This I did not take lightly. I don't think George did either, as his Dad and four uncles were all bush pilots in Alaska and all had been killed in plane crashes. As we sped down the runway, we soon came to the point of no return—we would have to clear the tops of those trees or die. We studied the tops of those trees just as we touched the tips with our landing gear and proceeded to climb. We didn't get 10 feet above those trees before three P-51 Mustang aircraft, flying low-level, crossed 50 feet above us doing about 350 mph. The noise, plus the tension we were already under, made that episode way too much. Those aircraft were, no doubt, on their way to the air show. We continued our trip, and landed in Pitt Meadows, B.C.. My cousin Richard picked us up and we spent the night at Uncle Bert's and Aunt Daisie's. The next day we were back to the airport and flew to Abbotsford. Once there, we met up with Cousins Pat, Norm, and Richard, and lifelong friend Jack. We enjoyed the air show, but soon got antsy about getting back to our base—something about being in a foreign country on a weekend that the Army knows nothing about.

There was one more flight of significance that we made from Ft. Lewis. Four of us flew from Ft. Lewis to Hayward, California. We flew in a single engine, low wing plane called a Navion. It was an interesting

trip; and once in California, we started following the Sacramento River. It wasn't long before we were in Hayward and landing. We were picked up and taken to Mom and Dad's in San Leandro. Of course we were fed well, and had a great visit; but it was soon time to go. Emmett and I picked up my Ford Skyliner and drove back to Ft. Lewis. George and the other pilot flew the plane back.

The Tour

One of Marty's friends, who soon became a friend of mine, was Carl. Carl had been stationed in Germany and drove an APC (armored personnel carrier). One evening as we sat playing cards, Carl asked Marty and I if we had ever been in an APC. Of course we said no, and I admitted I didn't even know what one was. His solution was to go down to the motor pool and get in one. Of course it was at night and the motor pool was closed. It was amazing to me that anyone who knew how to operate one of these things could just open one up get inside and fire it up. This, Carl wasted no time in doing. I don't know who suggested it, but it wasn't long before we were flying through the forest and swampy pools seeing what this thing would do.
Whether we ended up at the Roy Tavern with that thing is not really clear at this time. We did, however, manage to get back to the base without being detected. This was a good thing because we would probably still be in jail.

CHAPTER

7

The winds of change...

Towards the end of the summer, there was a change in the wind, with rumors of a military division to be formed at the base. It turned out to be true, with the 4th Infantry Division forming in early fall. The Division included an aviation battalion of UH-1 (Huey) helicopters. I was assigned to A ompany, consisting of 25 Hueys. Those

of us who went through helicopter Cmaintenance were quickly assigned to new barracks. With that came new sergeants and warrant officers (pilots) and full officers. In the enlisted ranks we had helicopter mechanics (some of whom would become crew chiefs) and gunners. The latter being infantry soldiers who were assigned to maintain and man the M-60 machine guns the helicopters would eventually have. The job of organizing and training these new mechanics and crew chiefs was not an easy one. The fellow that had that job was extremely particular—maybe even to a fault. However he did what he felt he had to do.

I don't know how they chose who was to be a crew chief, and who was going to be a mechanic; but I was assigned as a mechanic. I should mention that a mechanic worked on all the aircraft, while the crew chief was assigned to a particular helicopter. A lot of fellows would lose the desire to be a crew chief and fly with the helicopter, when we got to Vietnam.

Our Division got orders to deploy to the central highlands of Vietnam. Our job, at that point, was to prepare the helicopters for the trip.

The attack…

Months went by with training and participating in combat exercises. One exercise in particular was another of those bivouac things that I seemed to have trouble with. I have to say at this point that any trouble at this outing was solely my own undertaking. We set our camp up in the "rain forest" of Washington State. To those unfamiliar with Washington State, using the term "rain forest" seems redundant. The idea was that we would set up a perimeter defense, and wait to be attacked. In the mean time, the cooks set their big general-purpose tent and cooking lines to conduct business. Camp being set up. We waited. We waited some more. Part of this game included referees and weapons with blank cartridges. I never saw the black and white striped shirts, but they were there just the same. Their job was to tag anybody who was out in the open when the "attack" came. *I wonder if any one can read my mind at this point?*

Just how long were we supposed to sit here doing nothing? After all, didn't we have to earn the money we were making—all $79 a month? Did I have to take matters into my own hands— apparently so? After all, we waited 3 days for something to happen. Then I had a thought…Maybe we should check our preparedness? I ran this past some of my colleagues and they agreed. Our strategy was for three of us to sneak out 100 yards or so into the trees, open fire on our camp, and sneak back. Those remaining on our defense line would return fire; the noise and commotion would cover our return to camp. They were notified of our departure, and we stealthily crept out in front of our company's position. It was not long before the shooting began. The plan was *almost* without fault. That is to say, we returned without being detected. To say the plan was faultless would not take into account the cooks' tent catching fire in the melee. It also would not take into account our Company Commander and First Sergeant being tagged as "dead" and sent back to our real base. Several others were tagged; but the issue was "preparedness," right?

Our return back from the "mission" was greeted by the regular troops as a total success. Therein lay the problem. Who can resist trying to at least repeat a "total success"? Not me! A second "mission" was planned 2 days later. The boys on the front lines were notified and three of us snuck off again. The same plan was executed, and we returned as before. As we came running back and fell down on the hillside in laughter; I looked up on the hill above us, and there stood Sergeant Klink. The joke was over at that point. The price was yet to be paid. The original troops who were supposed to "attack," never showed up. Did the military know us so well that they knew we would provide our own attack? Wow, how scary is that? The other question is: Did the attacking force hear of our foray; and if so, how? I think those stinking referees were working for the other side.

At any rate, we moved camp in the middle of the night "just because." It might not have been so bad except it was pouring down rain. Taking down what was left of the cooks' tent gave me a little twinge. How could *they* let that happen? In the middle of all this packing stuff up and pouring rain, a Warrant Officer came up to me and asked, "When was the last time you shaved soldier?" All sorts of disrespectful thoughts ran through my head. It wasn't like I was some sort of hairy guy that needed to shave every few hours. And why did he choose to ask me? Was he picking on me? After all, what did I do?

We ended up going back to Fort Lewis and I thought, "Working with these fly boys was going to be okay."

CHAPTER

8

The big green pond...

We went back to preparing the helicopters for the trip across the big green pond. We had a 2-week break at Christmas where we all went home. Upon returning, last preparations were made and on January 8, 1967 we shipped out. Most of our company was sent over on a jet, (commercial) the rest of us went on a flat top aircraft carrier that was run by the "Merchant Marines." Now the aircraft carrier was probably used to fly the old bi-planes off of because a normal aircraft could not fly off it; it was too short. I also meant to  indicate the age of this thing. The name of this ship was the USS Kula Gulf. It turns out that Marty ended up going over on the same ship some months later. Initially, as the ship left the Seattle area, the weather and the seas were rough. This did not sit well with a bunch of landlubbers. As each day passed, more and more guys became seasick. One fellow in our Company had the dubious distinction of getting the nickname of *Puke*. It was probably ten days before the seas settled down, and we became accustomed to the motion and the awful smell of the diesel motors. Besides his face could not stay green forever.

The military, I discovered, does not believe in cruise ships. *Idle hands are not happy hands.* We were assigned bunks in the belly of this whale and were shown the facilities. The bunks were stacked four high, with about 18 inches between them. The worst part being that you could not even rollover with someone in the bunk above. The sit-down bathroom consisted of a trough about 12 feet long at which a piece of pipe was welded on the front and back. The toilet seat was a sliding 2-part effort. It was set up for six users on each side with the isle in the center. The beauty of this was it could take up to a 6-foot wide butt…if it had to. Through these troughs was pumped salt water that ran constantly. The disconcerting thing about this picture, as I found out, was that if you were up stream, there were those who would analyze your last meal. Not a pretty picture.

CHAPTER

9

Pre-Camo…

For those who did not have duty on a particular day, we were assigned to go to P.T. (physical training). We were supposed to have shined boots, starched shirts and pants, and a shiny brass belt buckle. As I said earlier, this was no cruise ship, and it had a distinct lack of facilities. For example, how were we supposed to have starched anything? And how were we supposed to even iron shirts or pants? It just wasn't possible, so we took a different tack. Now I'd been thinking, from what I had seen so far with this Army stuff, they didn't *seem* to be overly concerned about my welfare. Maybe I was going to have to make some command decisions.

And so it was done, for better or worse. This approach was a burr in the saddle for those who commanded me. I considered it looking ahead. The main thing that we did was soak our brass belt buckles in salt water. The purpose of this, of course, was to turn the buckle green. This we figured would make us less visible to those who didn't know us, but wanted to harm us anyway. And it goes without saying that shining our boots was out of the question. Now the belt buckle issue created certain problems. The first being, our pants would fall down. We allowed them down to a certain point because our shirts weren't tucked in. To go along with this California-look, we left our boots undone also. At first, second, and third glance this appeared "sloppy". What they did not appreciate was that this look was temporary. You can't hurry corrosion. Don't ask where we got the salt water! All of this created an image the "higher ups" did not appreciate. Who would have guessed that the Army would later come out with a green "camouflage" belt buckle? We also had to come up with a way to stay out of sight for a while. We did the only sensible thing; we hid! This worked great for some time. There were lots of historic things to explore on this fine vessel. I was looking for the oarlocks, but never did find them. There were a lot of good hiding places.

We were finally forced to the surface one evening, when at a formation, the sergeant stated that at P.T. there was only one guy from our company. OOOOOh! As a result, "All you guys that didn't have duty were to start washing all 25 of our helicopters." The guys that had duty came to us and said they'd help. So all of us enlisted guys, minus one (guess who), started washing. At the time, we were going through the Philippine Islands. It was very hot after being used to Washington State in January. So we stripped down to our fatigue pants and washed and washed. As a team, we worked great. In 3½ hours, we were done. The sergeant was summoned. He surveyed the situation at a distance of 50 feet to the closest helicopter and said, "You couldn't have washed them all in that amount of time, wash 'em again." At this point, the volunteers gracefully bowed out, and we were left to our own devices. It was 9:30 at night, and we were tired. We proceeded on until about 11:30; then quit. We had been sleeping up on the deck in the open fresh air so it was a relief to get back up there. The fellow that had made the complaint about the lack of companionship at PT decided to bring his mattress, pillow, blankets and sheets up on deck with the rest of us. This proved to be a tactical error on his part. He returned down into the bowels, I suppose to get his *teddy bear*. When he returned, his mattress, pillow, blankets and sheets were gone. I think some Philippino family got a late but soggy Christmas present. The next day we made time to go to PT. Funny how things work. After PT we got to lounge on deck in the tropical sun, and smell the wondrous smells coming from those islands.

Overboard...

There was a tech sergeant on board who we felt was beyond reasonable in his approach to what we had to do. He was lying on deck asleep a few feet from me. I raised my head to look, and two others did the same at the same time. It was as though the three of us had the same dream. We all jumped up and grabbed the sleeping tech's arms and legs. We then began swinging him over the side. On the chance you've ever awakened to find yourself looking down at the ocean going by 30 feet under you, I think you can imagine the effect. On the count of three we dropped him to almost deck height, then pulled him in. We put him back down on the deck and let go. He got up, looked at us with glazed eyes, and then walked off. That guy became the best-darned Tech Sergeant we ever had!

The Tour

CHAPTER

10

The War...

Before long we sailed into Vung Tau harbor, near Saigon. That night, as we peered out at the flares going off and heard the artillery booming in the darkness, we could imagine the fighting going on and the poor souls involved. Soon it would be us, we thought. The next day was filled with getting helicopters ready to fly off the deck of this flat top. All the preparation for transporting the helicopters had to be undone. It was a time-consuming process. Apparently I had made quite an impression on a sergeant from another company who was on the ship, even though I had never before seen this guy. As I was working on a helicopter, he came up to me and said "Bain, before we get out of here, I am going to have your ass." Here was another guy that did not respect the property rights of the U.S. Government. *Do I have to educate all these guys?* I informed him that he would need to bring some extra lunch with him if he wanted that to happen. Needless to say, I missed out on making a good friend that day. I could tell by how red his face got as he stormed off!

The Tour

Borrow A Bullet?

The next morning brought a change I doubt I'll ever forget. After initially having to work on helicopter preparations, I was called down to go on a mission. My friend Dick and I were to get our M-14s, backpacks, and canteens, then proceed to the flight deck. We were told we would be flown to an airfield, walk to the beach, and guard two sea containers. As we lifted off the deck in one of our Hueys, I could not help feeling something was not right—we had no ammo and no provisions. While in the air, they pointed out these containers on the beach—they appeared to be about ¼ mile from the airfield. Upon landing, we approached the guard shack at the perimeter, and noticed there was an American and a Vietnamese guard. Dick spoke to the American. He said, "Say buddy we just got to this country, and heard there was a war on." Pausing, he added, "I wonder if we could borrow a bullet." The reply from our comrade in arms was, "Sorry, I'm not authorized." This certainly fit. It was going to be a long year. The ridiculousness of our situation hit me. Here we were, in a war zone. We were given no bullets, no water, no food, no shelter, no sleeping bags, and no instructions as to how long this craziness was going to go on. Dick thanked the soldier, and off we went.

Upon leaving the airfield, we crossed the street and proceeded towards the containers. We didn't get 100 feet before a small 3-wheeled vehicle stopped beside us. It had three occupants. A woman jumped out and put a wok-size container on the ground at our feet. She immediately jumped back in the vehicle, and they prepared to leave. Dick and I looked at each other, knowing the possibilities, and started running down the road.

We were left out there for 5 days, as all of our "forward thinking" put us in disfavor. Imagine that! We found food, we found water, and we found a bullet. What we did not find was relief from the unrelenting sun. After a couple days our faces were blistered. Coming from Washington State in early January to this tropical climate had a price, and we were paying it. Just as difficult as the sun were the nights. We had to lie on top of the containers, which were cold anyway, but the moisture in the air seemed to make it rain on us. All we had to cover ourselves was a poncho liner. As for sleep, there wasn't much of that, just because it was so uncomfortable. I believe we would have given away whatever was in those containers if someone would have pointed a gun at us. After all, if the Army didn't care enough to give us a bullet, how were we going to fight anybody?

After 5 days, our boys came to get us. We were told we would be flying to our base in the "central highlands" the next morning. Meeting our friends was a relief after the 5 days of isolation. What a strange country this seemed to be. There were, however, wondrous smells that were totally new. The small billowy clouds on the bright blue sky highlighted the dark green foliage. Being a 19-year-old and only living in two very similar countries, Canada and the good old USA, this country seemed disorganized and chaotic. Of course there was a war going on and some people were given bullets.

The Tour

CHAPTER

11

The Hand Gun Decision…

Our flight up to our base camp (Camp Enari) took the better part of a day. Arriving late in the afternoon, we were hustled off where we were assigned a general-purpose tent to live in. We were also reconnected with our clothing and miscellaneous other equipment. Meeting up with the rest of our comrades was enjoyable as there were lots of stories to be exchanged. One of the items of news was that one of our gunners had been shot. Apparently, two gunners had been drinking and decided to play Russian roulette. At that point in time, all helicopter crewmembers carried side arms. The idea was, in case they were shot down, they would have extra protection. So, in their drunken stupor they were trying to see who could shoot the other .It turns out they both lost. One was paralyzed from the neck down; the other was arrested and put in a sea container for who knows how long. The tragedy was that they were good friends. I hope none of us have friends like that. The result of this incident was that all side arms were taken away from the crew chiefs and gunners. Apparently, the enlisted types are not responsible enough to carry side arms.

The Tour

Our Base for a Year…

The tent where the cooks slept was fitted with a .50-caliber machine gun—the head cook had been to Vietnam before and had contacts. I didn't think it was the time to tell them, "Sorry about your cook tent back in Washington." Discretion being an appropriate survival method, like preparedness, but dissimilar to "forward thinking". The tent where we slept was on the perimeter of the base. The only thing separating us from the guard bunkers was a road that surrounded the base. It, of course, was just a dirt road that had very little traffic, which was a good thing.

Because to urinate, we needed to cross the road, stand in the open, and pee into a tube that was stuck in the ground. While standing there you could see for miles into the valley. It was okay though, because if there were any enemy snipers out there, at least you would die getting some kind of relief.

The base was about a half-mile square with our company making up the east perimeter. Further east was the city of An Khe, and east of that was the port city of Quin Nhon. The infantry occupied the south perimeter, and their camp backed up to the steel plate runway that we had.

The runway was only 2800 feet long, so very few fixed-wing aircraft landed there. The runway ran from east to west. It did however get a lot of helicopter traffic. The northern area of the base was occupied by the

Headquarters of the 4th Infantry Division. I believe the artillery unit occupied the western end of the base. To the west of us was Firebase Oasis; even further west was the Cambodian border. North of us was the city of Pleiku with its good-sized runway. Further north of that was Dak To, an area that was both mountainous and deadly. Our camp, because of all the tents, looked rather primitive. In fact it was! Looking at this camp and realizing that we had to stay here for a year, left an empty feeling in my stomach. How could we put up with living in this dirt for a year? It was going to be tough.

Before the monsoons some of us would go outside and get a game of tag football going. We could normally find 10-12 guys willing to play. We had an area in our Company that was big enough to play a game. It wasn't level and it was just dirt that was a little rough, but we had fun.

Doing Our Job...

So we settled in to our maintenance routine with the Hueys needing inspection every 25 flying hours. That was about 2 - 2 ½ days of flying. Within a week, we were up to our eyeballs in work. The way the system worked was that we would do the 25-, 50- and 75-hour maintenance requirements. A higher echelon team performed the 100-hour checks.

To lighten our day, Mike would wait until some sergeant was watching him, then he'd start walking towards another helicopter or one of our tent-type hangers. All of a sudden, he would trip and fall flat on his face. There would be billows of dust surround him and for 15-20 seconds, and he would not be seen. When the dust cleared, he would get up, dust himself off, and walk on as if nothing happened. He had perfected the move to a "T". The sergeants would just shake their heads and walk off. We of course, would laugh. We never did make up any scorecards, although it would have been appropriate.

As time went on and our pilots tried to push the envelope of what our helicopters could carry, there was occasionally a problem. One of our pilots tried to take off somewhat overloaded and as he dipped the nose to get forward momentum the skid caught the steel plate runway and tore the skids off. This was not good—now he had no way to land. He proceeded to get rid of his cargo, and refueled in a hover. This hadn't been done before for safety reasons. Now we had to find an extra set of skids to bolt back on while he hovered several feet off the ground. The job got done before he ran out of fuel, and the pilot was glad to be back on the ground. I was to have another adventure with the same pilot months later when I became a crew chief.

Preparedness Check- Again...

A strange tradition had been started sometime before I arrived at this base. At 9:00pm every night, those on guard duty would open fire with whatever weapon was at their post. I immediately recognized this as a preparedness check. The only difference was they were using real bullets. Cool!!! I certainly saw the value in it. After all, who would want to approach a base at night manned by a bunch of crazies? This process seemed to work as this base was not attacked during my tour.

The Tour

The Coast...

My first trip to the coast was done in the back of 2½-ton truck (called a deuce and a half) set up with benches. It was interesting to see the people, and the greenest fields I had ever seen. The rice paddies were dark green and obviously taken care of very well. Our distrust of the people made us keep a watchful eye on everyone. We were green as grass and it was easy to see. Our trip there and back was done in a convoy to give us the most protection possible. We were even given real bullets. They must not have known I was in the bunch. The trip was mostly uneventful, and the evening found us in Quin-Nhon. We slept wherever we could, and proceeded back to our base the next day. Going up the pass was extremely slow, as those trucks will only do 5mph up a steep grade. This is the same mountain pass that the 1st Air Cav (Cavalry) fought for, just 6 months before. I hope the enemy isn't a sore loser. We were all glad to get back to the safety of our base even though I enjoyed the scenery.

The Natives...

Our base, being in the central highlands, had a look similar to California—rolling hills with golden brown grass; the gullies occasionally having bushes and trees. There were areas with stands of trees, just not at our base. One area that had trees was about a half mile from us, and occupied by the Montagnard tribes people. They were an interesting people that seemed to be out-of-place. Their facial features resembled some of our Native Americans. In fact, they were a fairly handsome people. They lived in bamboo huts that were rectangular in shape and set about 4 feet off the ground. Most were about 60 feet long and about 20 feet wide. To keep them dry, the roof was thatched with palm fronds. The people, themselves, seemed somewhat primitive to us. They grew what they needed, and were mostly self-sufficient. One could not help but notice that the women of the tribe went around topless. And we thought they were primitive. It was like going to a beach near San Francisco. A strange thing to me was the houses always faced the same direction. Other tribal huts in other locations faced the same direction. I don't know if it had to do with the weather or if it was some spiritual thing. We had a regular trip out there to help with anything that might have needed tending to. The intended purpose was for medical aid. Why they sent a bunch of soldiers along, I don't know; but it could have been for the purpose of security. They were a friendly people that welcomed us each time we came. Why would we consider them primitive when they were self-sufficient, did not adversely affect their environment, and had lived in the same spot for years? This is something we still don't have a handle on. One of the things they grew that I got to sample was a pineapple—it was the best I have ever tasted.

The Lawn...

My next trip to the coast was rather different. It started out with me driving that deuce and a half. I had to go to the motor pool where they issued me a license. After picking up the truck, I returned to our Company to pick up the guy who was going to be riding shotgun for me.

The Tour

Now I must point out that this guy is supposed to protect me if we come under attack. So after picking this guy up and driving to Pleiku where the convoy was forming up, we waited. There was a flurry of activity, as the locals tried to sell various items to us GIs waiting. As we sat there, I watched a Vietnamese woman eat her lunch. She had rice and some fish. The thing I had trouble with, was the flies that landed on her food; and she proceeded as if they were never there. I never got used to that.

While I watched all this, my trusty shotgun-guy asked a local to come to the truck. When she jumped on the running board, he asked her if she had any grass. She then disappeared and came back a couple minutes later and handed him a bag full of seeds. He paid her and the transaction was complete. Now, I had been playing football at the compound and had several scrapes to prove it. What could be better than some green grass to play on? So I asked, "What are you going to do with that?" He looked at me incredulously, he said, "You smoke it man; you smoke it." My hopes were instantly dashed, and my disappointment might have showed. I am sure he was thinking, "This guy is some kind of country pumpkin." Okay! Okay! But I hadn't lived out in the country in years. The lines were now drawn; and this guy that my life depended on, was not looking real dependable.

The convoy finally got under way and the mountain pass loomed ahead. Nearly 1500 French soldiers lost their lives in this pass. This was somewhat disconcerting to me the closer we got to it. Of course, the guy riding with me is genuinely "happy." Oh boy! We made it through the

The Tour

mountains okay and all the way to the coastal city of Quin-Nhon. The convoy dispersed; and the three trucks from our Company got loaded with materials, and were ready to go in a couple hours. This created a problem. It was getting dark, and none of us knew where the return convoy was to form up. One fellow, who seemed to know everything (just ask him), said he knew the way, and led the three trucks out of town. It wasn't long before nothing looked familiar. It also wasn't long before darkness fell. We drove for at least 2 hours not really knowing where we were going. It was no secret that the daytime and the night were two totally different animals in Vietnam—people and soldiers sometimes had a tendency to "change sides." This possibility did not escape me as we came into a village that was full of armed soldiers. Our leader apparently asked how to get to An Khe, the town on our way back to Camp Enari. He was greeted with a laugh, as they told him we'd been going the wrong direction ever since we left Quin-Nhon. So for 2 more hours in darkness, we had those trucks pressed to the limit, trying to get back alive. We finally got back to Quin-Nhon without losing anybody. We slept on the top of our load, of course, no sleeping bags or even poncho liners. "Plan ahead" comes to mind. We were lucky to have survived that foray. Next time may not be that lucky. The enemy would have liked to have that material our trucks were loaded with, I'm sure of that. The next morning we found a convoy for the trip back to Camp Enari. That was lucky as there was no one place or company or authority, that we were aware of, that set up convoys. So from our perspective, it was pure luck. Back at camp, our routine was back to normal. Why I got picked for these trips to the coast I can only guess.

  The floor of our tent was a series of pallets stacked side by side. Rather difficult to walk on and also a good collector of any sort of miscellaneous stuff. One night as sleep descended on me, I awoke in the middle of the night to hear a baby screaming. This startled me out of a deep sleep. I shined my flashlight in the direction of the noise only to realize that the noise was not a baby, but a rat. My options at this point seemed limited. The only thing available to me was a bayonet that I kept under my pillow. Being on the top bunk made it a little easier to "let fly" the old bayonet, so that's what I did. I had never heard a rat laugh before then. It was far better than the scream he had been producing. He did decide to vacate the premises shortly thereafter and I went back to a nervous sleep.

It seems my popularity with the powers that be was growing in leaps and bounds. I was about to experience one of the jobs that I was apparently well suited for. The job was that of a "shit stirrer." Now, I had been called one; but to actually have the job… Wow! What was involved was to pull the 50 gallon drums that were cut in half from the back of the outhouse, pour in some diesel fuel, and (here's the best part) stir it. It was then necessary to light the mixture on fire. The job was to last all-day; so, in the time necessary to wait for more stirring or more fuel to be added, I could do whatever I wanted. I used the time to write letters, listen to music, or sit in the sun and do both. By this time in my tour, I had already purchased a big Akai reel-to-reel tape recorder that came with two 2-foot tall speakers. So with the recordings I made, I could kick back and listen to some really nice sounds. This actually made for a relaxing day if not somewhat smelly. To those who received letters, I neglected to tell them not to smell them, although one time should cure them of that. Oh well, it's not a perfect world.

The Tour

CHAPTER

12

The Coke Attack…

My next trip to the coast was about to begin. This time, my good friend Dick was going to be riding shotgun. If you recall, he was the "Can I borrow a bullet?" guy. He was about my height, and build. He had thick blonde hair that made him look like a surfer. He was educated, as he had several years of college. He also had an A&P license—this was an aircraft mechanics license. He was, therefore. drafted into the infantry. Go figure! Dick was employed by United Air Lines as a mechanic before being drafted. I found his laid-back wit most entertaining.

We made it to Pleiku, waiting for some time for a convoy to form up. We headed again through the mountain pass for Quin Nhon. The trip was uneventful. Our truck was loaded again, and off we went—this time in the right direction. Darkness was approaching, so we stopped at an American base for the night. In the morning, we asked around for any knowledge of a convoy. No luck. No one seemed to know anything about convoys, so a decision had to be made. I must point out that on these trips we had no way of communicating with anyone. There were no radios for us truck driving types. We decided we would get into more trouble if we waited around hoping for a convoy than if we just took off for our base. So off we went. One truck traveling alone in a country being infiltrated by the enemy almost everywhere we looked.

The Tour

Everything went fine until we got into the steep section of the mountain pass with the truck only doing 5mph. As we rounded one particular corner, there were two soldiers walking along each side of the road ahead. They were both carrying rifles and were obviously not American, but what were they? Our lives hung in the balance. Dick's rifle was beside him; but because of the close quarters, was unable to get it at-the-ready. We approached even closer, and the soldier on my side put up his hand for us to stop. At least he didn't shoot us. So I figured maybe he was a *friendly*. He did not look Vietnamese. His face was round and he was fairly stocky. He was either North Vietnamese (I hadn't seen one), or from another country. I stopped, and he indicated he wanted a ride. He hopped on the running board and his partner did the same thing on Dick's side. Off we went. This was a tremendous relief as both guys had to sling their rifles over their shoulders. It would have been impossible to shoot us from this position. We must have traveled 10 miles with those guys hanging onto the doors. Why I didn't figure out who these guys were, I don't know; but I was about to find out.

We approached a town, and I started slowing down. As we crossed the bridge into town, it occurred to me who these fellows might be. The Korean "Tiger Division" occupied this area. We had worked with this Division before, and they had a reputation for being ruthless. The fellow on my side indicated he wanted me to stop. Stop I did. He jumped off; the guy on the other side did the same.

There were people camped at the river. There were foxholes, tents, and a command post. Soldiers were milling about. As the guy on my side's feet hit the ground, there was an explosion that was extremely close and we could feel it in the truck. His eyes got big as saucers. People were jumping in the river, soldiers jumping in foxholes, guys looking for their rifles; it was pandemonium. I yelled at Dick, "They're

The Tour

being mortared." I shoved the truck into gear, and down the road we flew. That truck speedometer went to sixty and was pegged. It must have been quite a sight. The road was full of potholes and that truck ran like a thoroughbred with its only occasionally tires touching the road.

After an hour, we finally arrived at a small town and I needed to stop. A thirst had been acquired in that episode. I began looking for the can of Coke that I had purchased at the coast. It was set between the canopy and the seat I was sitting on. It was nowhere to be found. Not under the seat, not behind the seat, not on the other side of the truck. I was baffled. Finally I looked under

the truck. There, wedged between the spare tire and the exhaust pipe was my can of Coke. The end was blown out. It had apparently heated up and exploded when we stopped at the bridge at An Khe. I wonder if those people running for the foxholes and jumping in the river would have found that amusing. I didn't go back to ask them! I would have felt very sheepish even asking . Our trip back to Camp Enari from that point was uneventful.

The Attitude Adjustment…

Dick and I were sent on one more trip to the coast. This time we had one other truck from our Company. It was driven by Felipe. Felipe was a nice young guy of Mexican decent. He was extremely polite and soft spoken. He was also about 5 feet tall and weighed about 100 lbs. His

The Tour

shotgun for this trip was John. John was a stocky guy and weighed about 180lbs. We had an uneventful trip down; but once we got there, things started to happen. We needed to kill some time, so three of us decided to see if we could find the USO Club - the forth of our contingent decided to go to the closest bar. I must explain at this point that the USO was a safe haven for soldiers who had some time off. It really was like going to the library in the U.S. in some respects. The bar on the other hand was more of a free-for-all—anything could happen.

The three of us returned to see how our load was coming, only to meet up with John who started demanding that Felipe give him some money. Felipe insisted that he did not have any money. John insisted again, this time more belligerent. Again Felipe said he had none. John then swung and hit Felipe in the mouth. Instantly I was mad, so I stepped in front of Felipe and told John to leave him alone. John said, "So do you want some?" meaning a punch in the face. He instantly swung at me and missed. I swung at him and didn't miss. He fell to the ground. He got back up and came at me again. I hit him a second time. This time he went down face first in 4 inches of powdered dirt. He was spread-eagle on the ground and he wasn't moving. We did something at this point that we should never have done. We left him there. So off we go back to the USO Club with the idea that we would give him ten minutes or so to gather himself and perhaps have a better attitude. Wrong!

When we returned John was gone. An American came up to us and asked if we were looking for a guy of John's description. Of course we said yes. At that point he informed us that John had been arrested and taken to jail. "For what?" we asked. It seems that when he got up, he decided to go into the closest bar and tear it up. So much for a 'better attitude.' We had no choice but to take off without him and head back to the highlands. We had a safe trip back although again we had no convoy.

The Tour

The next day I heard that the company commander had to send a chopper down to the coast to pick up John, and he was mad about it. I thought at this point if the C.O. wanted to get me, this would be a good chance for him. The Company never even questioned me about what happened; nor did they question Dick. Hey, they missed their chance.

The Tour

CHAPTER

13

The Mail...

Back at camp we resumed our normal duties. No one ever asked us what took so long, or how we got back so fast. It's almost like nobody knew we were gone. I'm sure they did though, because there wouldn't have been anybody to stir the poop.

Back on the flight line, at the end of the day, one of the office staff came to me and gave me a note. It was delivered by a pilot of an OV-1B Mohawk who had landed at our airstrip. It was from Marty, saying he was stationed near the coast and he and all his pals were okay. Apparently Marty was the crew chief of this particular aircraft, and talked the pilot into dropping off the note. The Mohawk was one of about four fixed wing aircraft that the Army had. It was used for reconnaissance, and had some armament capabilities. The other fixed-wing of note was the Caribou. It was a cargo and troop transport. Apparently the guy who complained about the lack of companionship at PT had a brother in the Air Force, because someone complained that the Army had airplanes and so those were taken away and given to the Air Force.

One day, one of the helicopters I had worked on did a run-up (started the turbine engine) and discovered a fuel leak. It turns out that I forgot to put the new "O" rings in the fuel filter. This could have been a catastrophic event for the crew. Thankfully, they followed procedures and caught it. This particular event would change my direction for the next eight months.

The Oasis...

Another road trip I had to make was out to a firebase. This was a base that was about 7 miles removed from base camp that had several artillery pieces capable of firing to locations closer to where the enemy may be. On this occasion we drove out there, dropped off what they needed, and then started back. There happened to be a nice stream part way back. Several of us decided to go for a swim. Being a country boy (bumpkin), this was a natural thing. We spent an hour swimming and fooling around. Our rifles were kept close, but not always right-at-hand. When we got back to base camp we heard the news. It seems the enemy attacked that firebase, and tried to over-run it. We must have been so close to being in the mix that, even today, it is scary to think about that day.

The Monsoons...

The monsoons were about to start; and the dust that made ripples as you walked, was about to turn to ankle deep mud. Our life, because of the monsoons, was going to change for the worse. After working all day and wanting to take a shower, it wasn't just the rain you had to deal with. But once you took a shower, you had to walk back in the mud to get to your tent. If you didn't slip and fall, only your feet and lower legs would be dirtier than when you left. At about 3000-foot elevation, it was not warm when it rained. Once you were wet, that was it. Cold set in. There was a distinct lack of rain gear for this elevation.

Normally after working all day, we would go back to our tents; and at a specified time, there would be a formation. We would all line up, the Sarge would say a few words, and we would march over to the mess tent. This was only done in times of harassment, which was about half the time. This type of thing was almost unheard of in Vietnam. It stopped after the Company Commander Grenade Incident.

Once in the mess tent, we would go through the line and see if there was anything edible. Then we would get our bowl of tea—there were no glasses. We normally didn't eat much, so it wasn't long before we were back in our tents.

We had a club, of sorts, that sometimes had warm beer. *Any port in a storm* comes to mind! The only beer they had was called *Ballentine* beer. It was made in the Philippines. I suppose they were getting back at us for getting their bedding wet or maybe they were using that bedding to filter the beer. At any rate, for being the only game in town, that beer was not very popular. The officers, on the other hand, had a great club in which to enjoy their off-hours. It looked like it was built by the Montagnard tribes' people. It had bamboo walls and floor, and was built about 3 feet off the ground. The roof was made of palm fronds. It also had a deck that went around the whole structure. The whole thing looked very tropical, and was envied by us enlisted. One evening, a few of us lowly enlisted-types heard about a show the officers were having in their club. It turned out to be a strip show. As the show progressed, more and more enlisted heard about it, and swarmed onto the bamboo deck trying to get a peek through the bamboo. Just as things were getting really interesting, the deck collapsed and guys were flying everywhere. One of the guys yelled out "I saw her beaver. I saw her beaver." "She had a beaver with her?" I asked." "Maybe she's from Canada. Maybe I know her!" Most of us were feeling no pain at this point, so the collapse was hilarious. The officers, however, saw no humor in it; and demanded we get off what was left of the deck.

During the monsoons most guys would stay in their tents and write letters, play cards, or just shoot-the-bull.

Three Tango…

I had to make one more trip driving a deuce and a half. This time I went by myself, as I had to deliver some troops to a place called *3-Tango*, about 24 miles west of Pleiku, near the Cambodian border. Most helicopter crews did not want to fly to this place.

Their commanding officer rode in the front with me. We were passing a village when one of the troops in the back yelled we were being shot at. By the time he told us, we were already past the village. We proceeded on, as we had to get to 3-Tango before an aircraft. It was so far out in the sticks that the road was washed out in numerous places, and we came upon old French vehicles that had been blown up. The really surprising thing about this is that these vehicles had not been touched in all those years. I had never seen that in this country before.

We finally got there in the afternoon, and shortly thereafter a C-123 cargo plane landed on this runway in the jungle. There wasn't a building or any other form of human habitation anywhere to be seen. It was too late to return to the camp, so I had to spend the night with these infantry guys. Lots of stories were told about their encounters with the enemy. It did not escape me that we were close to the Cambodian border, and there were only about 15 of us to defend ourselves. This close to the border, if they (North Vietnamese) came, it would be en masse—maybe 100, or possibly 200 men. It was not a comfortable night for me.

    I did not know what our procedures were if we got attacked. Why were we even out here? I did not know the answer to these questions. We made it through the night okay. The next day, I had to drive back to base camp by myself. This, I was not comfortable with. I believe I was feeling the effects of "forward thinking." I made it back to camp okay, if not somewhat nerved. And to think, I'm was not even a citizen and going through all this. There were a few times I said, "Canada, here I come!" Although Canada was getting a bad name because of all the draft dodgers going up there just to avoid this kind of fun.

The Tour

CHAPTER 14

Back at camp and trying to settle in again. I decided to take a shower. As I walked past Second Platoon's tent, a shot rang out and a bullet whizzed past my head. It seems E-4 Hone was inside the tent cleaning a captured AK-47, and he forgot to check to see if it was loaded. It might have been safer for me on the road. Specialist 4 Millard C. is a story unto its own. As a 17-year veteran of military duty, he was the same rank as I. He became a crew chief; and during his service in Vietnam, was shot down and/or his helicopter crashed three times. That, however, was not what got him. He eventually came down with malaria, and was sent home.

The Oscar...

As the Company stood in formation one day, the sergeant stood in front and stated the business of the day. That being complete, he proceeded to tear into my friend Robert. He said, "Robert, you're a trouble maker," and continued from there to belittle him. He then jumped to Dick. He said "Dick, you're smart, but you are too damned smart for your own good." He continued to tear into him. He then turned to me and said, "Bain, you're the worst of them all," and proceeded to tell us all what he thought of me. He then dismissed the Company. I cannot tell you how many guys turned around and shook my hand and said, "Congratulations, you win." It made the whole event more palatable, even funny. The strange thing was that, prior to my winning the Oscar, the only time I ever saw the sergeant was at formations. Why I got the highest honor, I have no idea.

George...

There were also others who did not care for me. Hard to believe, I know. One evening, as Dick and I sat talking, we were called to come over to one of the other tents. As we entered, we were met by one of our comrades, Phillip. He was apparently very drunk, in high state of irritation, and armed with a loaded M-14 rifle. We had been set up! He proceeded to tell us that he overheard us talking about him drinking too much and becoming a drunk. All the while, he had the rifle pointed at us and was intending to shoot. Enter our friend, George, who bravely stepped in front of us and asked Phillip to give him the gun. Phillip resisted, but George calmly talked to him some more. "Phil, you don't want to do this." A dozen men stood around and watched this play out. Our lives hung in the balance. George was an Eskimo from Nome, Alaska. He was short, but stocky, and liked by everyone. He was also respected by all. After about 5 minutes, Phillip handed the rifle over to George. We cheated death another day. George saved our lives. When Phil was told the next day what he did, he gave up drinking for some time, and apologized to Dick and myself. You will recognize Phillip when you get to the Sgt. Correia story.

The Tour

Snoopy...

William Biever was a South Dakota farm boy who had a college education with a degree in agriculture. He was friendly, amiable, and quick to smile. Everybody in the Company liked him. He was a crew chief in the Second Platoon. He didn't complain about his job, or how dangerous it was.

One mission that our crews had to fly was called a "Snoopy" mission. This flight was done flying low-level—just above the treetops. The helicopter was fitted with a machine that detected smoke and ammonia, the ammonia being given off in perspiration. The machine had an operator who was fitted with a radio transmitter, and who would call out a reading if there was one. The co-pilots would mark these readings on a map. This was later used at infantry headquarters. To round this system off, helicopter gun ships followed us. If there was trouble, or if we were shot down, the gun ships were there to bail us out and give us cover.

One fateful day, Bill Biever and the crew of his ship were given this mission in an area called Dak-To. This was an area that consisted of a narrow valley, surrounded by mountains. It was evacuated during monsoons, and we would fight to get it back when the monsoons ended. It was notorious as a bad place to be. As Bill's chopper flew up and down those mountains and hills, they started receiving fire. Bill was hit, but he continued to instruct the pilot to a landing spot as their chopper was going down. They hit the ground and the chopper rolled. Bill was killed. He was a true hero in my book. The rest of the crew got out alive. This was our Company's first loss. It was tragic. It was sobering. There was more to come.

The Tour

The next morning, as we were standing in formation, we could not help but notice our First Sergeant leaning against a water trailer. He had passed out, drunk out of his mind, and wet from urinating on himself. The other NCO's ignored him. This old sergeant was nice enough, and had a trademark salute—he was missing all but his thumb and baby finger on his right hand. It was a Hawaiian salute (as in hang loose). Apparently, the First Sergeant missed Bill, too.

That day there was a mission out to where Bill's helicopter had crashed. The purpose was to look for Bill's body. Specialist Omdahl lowered down on a rope to try to find Bill. It was an exceptionally brave thing to do as the enemy had lots of time to get to the site and set up an ambush. Omdahl only had two days left in country.

For Bill...

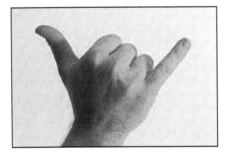

CHAPTER

15

Being a Crew Chief...

I was told the 3rd platoon had an opening for a crew chief. I talked the Platoon Leader, Capt. Don Files, and he said he'd make the arrangements for me to switch jobs. Apparently my maintenance leaders didn't mind me leaving. What a surprise! There was no cake, no good wishes, and no more stirring poop.

The flight-day normally began at 5:30am on the flight line. Crew chiefs would pre-flight the ship. The gunner got the guns, mounted them on the gun mounts, and prepared the ammunition. The pilots would come after the mission was assigned, and would do a run-up to check the turbine engine for any problems. After that, we were normally on our way. We usually did not return until 6:00-7:00pm. By then, the mess hall was shut down. Lucky for us!

The helicopters we flew in were called "Slicks," because all we had for armament were the two M-60 machine guns. The gunships on the other hand, were armed with rockets, sometimes grenade launchers; and the door-gunners had M-60 machine guns. Some of the door-gunners also carried M-79 grenade launchers (shotgun-type rifle that fired grenades). Gunships would lay a serious hurt on someone if they were the target.

The first few weeks as a crew chief was a blur, as the chopper I was to crew was in maintenance. When it came out, another platoon used it for the day, and it crashed. No one was hurt, but the chopper had to go back in to maintenance. When I was able to start flying, the monsoons were still going on. This meant flying low-level with the doors open, and manning the machine guns. Whenever possible, the pilots would fly around storm cells. Invariably, the gunner and I would get wet. Getting wet and flying at 100+ mph's tended to make one chilly. Downright cold even.

My first night at Firebase Oasis was cold and scary. I was wet and had no sleeping bag—no one told me we stayed overnight on these deals. At this firebase, they had a piece of artillery called the "Long Tom." It was the biggest artillery piece I had ever seen. As I was trying to sleep, this thing would fire. The noise was horrendous. The sides of the GP tent would shift over about 4 inches just from the concussion. It was hard to tell whether the noise was incoming or outgoing. Basically, I decided that if there were no troops yelling or running around, I'd just try to sleep. It made for a long night.

Re-Up...

Only once in my service-time did I hear of someone beating the Army at its own game. This was done by a guy, whose name I forget at this time. Convenient, huh? At any rate, he was a one of our gunners, was not a citizen, but had been drafted. He was within 6-months of getting out when he was asked if he wanted to re-up. They offered him $5000 and a 30-day leave. He took the $5000, took his 30-day leave, went back to Belgium, and never returned.

The Tour

Duds...

Back at Camp Enari a strange thing happened. Somebody hired some knot-head to throw a grenade into our Company Commanders' hooch (thatched hut), and also our Battalion Sergeant Major's hooch. The whole thing made for some initial excitement, but the grenades were duds. The result of all this was that all of our rifles were locked up at night. Most attacks by the enemy were done at night, so the logic of this move escapes me. I suppose logic has no part in war. Besides all this, the guy that had the key to the gun container was a drunk, and nobody could ever find him.

Now, I have failed to mention to you anything about the food. Before I go any further, I have to say the cooks did the best they could with what they were given. The breakfasts generally were inedible. The eggs they received were rotten and had no yolks. They were all milky-colored and stunk to high heaven. It seemed all the food they received was extremely poor quality. So the net result was there was a lot of trading going on with guys in the field. What those guys got, I do not know. Our guys got cases of "C" rations. These cases were stored in our lockers, and the meals eaten in our tents. Our friend, who was alone at PT on the ship, must have been alone one day at the mess hall and complained. The result was we were told that if we were caught with "C" rations in our lockers we would be court-martialed. This could result in jail time, loss of pay, and reduction in rank. All this over a can of ham and lima beans. Talk about a knee-jerk reaction! No wonder the Company Commander was dodging grenades.

The Tour

Charge Of Quarters…

One day after flying all day, I came back to the Company to find out that I had CQ that night. Upon checking with our office clerk, they had an IG (Inspector General) inspection the next morning. Of course, there was 6 months worth of paperwork to be caught up. He explained some of the things he needed done, and then left for the night. I worked all night trying to get this mess of paperwork done. Why I even tried I don't know. At 7:00am the next morning, the office clerk relieved me. Because there was an inspection that day, I was not allowed to go to sleep in my bunk. I mentioned to Capt. Files that I might as well crew my helicopter. He said okay, so off I went. It proved to be quite an awakening experience.

We left Camp Enari and went to a firebase where we picked up a long-range reconnaissance patrol team (LRRP). These guys, 3 Vietnamese and 1 American, were to be dropped off at some jungle location and survey the area for enemy activity. They were to be picked up in a couple of days after the initial drop-off. When we first picked them up, the American was on the right side of the chopper with the Vietnamese on the left.

Apparently the LZ (landing zone) was surveyed from 5,000 feet because the LZ was full of stumps and dead trees. (This survey was reportedly done by our grenade-dodging CO.) When we came in to land, the gunner and I had to direct the pilots where to put the tail boom. The tail rotor didn't like stumps—they made the chopper behave badly.

As the pilots held it at a hover about 6 feet off the ground, the Vietnamese started jumping out the left side; the American carrying the radio on his back followed. As he did, his radio bumped my radio in the helicopter, and turned my radio on to "private." Normally, this would not be a big deal. Today it was. I could not reach the radio switch from the cubby I sat at with the machine gun. I looked ahead of us, and at our 10 o'clock position was a big dead tree. The rotor blades seemed only a foot away.

I tried to warn the pilots. It was no use. No one could hear me unless their radio was on private. It only took a few seconds to drop the LRRP team, and the ship started going forward. Almost as quickly, the tree exploded as the rotor blades hit the tree. Our aircraft commander (A/C) yelled out that he could not control the helicopter. At almost the same time the LRRP team called out they were being shot at. This meant them coming back to the LZ and wanting us to pick them up. Our co-pilot, who was a former "Green Beret," said he had the controls. He was a cool customer. The ship had a bad vibration because the rotor blades were badly damaged. The AC radioed a "mayday." We began to pick up speed and gain a little altitude. They decided to stay low level in case the rotor blades came apart.

Other aircraft began to contact us wanting to know our position and status. We didn't know if our chopper was going to make it back to Camp Enari or not. The communications center back at camp heard what was going on. As we came in and landed safely, Capt. Files had two crew chiefs escort me back to camp. Why, I don't know. I wasn't hurt. I might have needed to change my shorts, but nobody helps with that. To this day, I don't know why the pilots didn't see that tree. They must have been focusing straight ahead. At any rate, I was allowed to go to bed, and the inspection was over - being up for 30 hours straight made me sleep well.

CHAPTER

16

Volunteering For R&R...

The helicopter was back in maintenance for new blades. I was back at camp on regular duty. One day in formation, the sergeant that honored me with "the worst of them all" asked the Company for 2 volunteers. Nobody budged. He repeated, "I'd like 2 volunteers for R&R." Nobody raised their hands. He stood there looking around at the Company giving us "the eye". Finally, Jerry and I looked at each other and nodded our heads. We then raised our hands. Obviously the mistrust kept everyone else from raising their hands.

The next day, Jerry and I were on our way to the Saigon area for a 3-day R&R. It was great to get away. Three days isn't much, but can lift the spirits a lot. On the first day in Saigon, Jerry and I were walking down a street and I heard someone call my name. Behind me was a guy I went to high school with and hung around with on occasions. What a small world. He was only going to be there for a couple days. Being there and seeing him was quite a coincidence.

Cutting the LZ...

Back at Camp Enari I was finally getting my ship back. It was a Huey "D" model, meaning it had an 1100 H.P. turbine motor. They were normally okay at sea level, but our base camp in the central highlands was nearly 3000 feet. When we re-supplied in the mountains, we were working at 5,000 feet and possibly more. These motors were not strong enough for carrying loads at that elevation. As we came to the edge of an LZ that was cut by hand on the side of a mountain, our rotor blades began chopping branches. The rain was falling hard, and the more we dropped in; the more power we seemed to lose. I could actually see the rotor blades slowing down. We were about 30 feet above the ground when the pilot said, "We're not going to make it; start throwing stuff out." All we had on board were some empty water cans and one soldier we picked up at another LZ. I swung myself around the seat post, and threw out the empty water cans. *Now what?*

I was not going to throw out the soldier. The AC decided we were going out of that LZ regardless of the consequences. He pulled up on the collective stick, and we started coming out. The co-pilot yelled, "We're over-torquing the rotor head." However, if the pilot had not done what he did, we would have crashed on that mountainside. As it was, we barely made it out. The power continued to drop until we cleared the trees and descended down the side of the mountain, hitting the tree tops with our skids as we picked up air speed.

Pie In The Sky...

I have to mention that I have tremendous respect for those poor guys in the infantry on the ground during the monsoons. They would be wet for weeks at a time. At times with "jungle rot" eating their flesh. They very seldom had hot meals—only when we would fly those meals out to them. On one such occasion, we were flying low-level with some hot chow in large insulated containers. There were mashed potatoes in one, meat in another, and apple pie in the third. Everything seemed to be going well as we got closer to our destination.

All of a sudden there was a loud noise. I didn't know what it was at first. The pilot was on the radio yelling, "Mayday! Mayday! This is Blackjack 613. I've been hit." This, of course, created a flurry of activity on the radio. In order to help the pilot, I swung around the seat post again—at 100+ mph this is not easy and definitely not safe. In doing this, I actually go outside the aircraft, only hanging on to the seat post; no safety lines or harnesses. So as I visually check the pilot, I see no sign of blood, a bullet, or any such thing. What I do find is apple pie scattered around the inside of the aircraft. The container lid had blown open and created the loud noise. This sent apple pie everywhere.

I imagined the pilot's embarrassment as he cancelled the mayday, and said he'd only been hit by "apple pie". We continued on the mission and delivered what was left of the apple pie.

Back at Camp Enari, walking through the mud was getting old. Electric cords lie in the mud and constantly short out the few lights that are strung up. It's very annoying if you're trying to write a letter. It's hard to stay clean with mud everywhere. Going on guard duty is a real pain this time of year. The wind and rain blow into the guard posts and the guy on guard gets wet while the guy sleeping tries to dry out. The 9:00pm shooting has been ordered stopped. No more letting the bullets fly.

Pilots…

There were certain pilots that were more enjoyable to fly with than others. One such pilot was Lt. Lovett. He had a great sense of humor and made the day easier to deal with. We could always count on him saying with a smile after a safe return, "We cheated death another day." That always brought a smile to my face.

Another pilot that I thought a lot of was Lt. Pavlicek. He seemed to have a good sense of humor and I got along with him well. He always wondered why I as a non-citizen was in Vietnam. He later transferred to "B" company (the gunship company) and was killed in action.

There were many more that I enjoyed flying with and have a great respect for them.

There was a pilot in our company that was in a crash and I ashamedly do not remember his name. We went to see him in the hospital in Pleiku and he was not in good shape. He had a head injury and was in a bed unconscious and wearing nothing but a diaper and a head wrap. He was in the fetal position and while we were there he never moved. I do not know whatever happened to him. All brave men doing a dangerous job.

CHAPTER 17

Misery...

The rain affected those out in the field far more than we even dreamed of. Those poor guys were wet for weeks not to mention the fact that the enemy might be behind the next tree. One day we got a call for a medivac to one of the company's we served. As we dropped in to the L.Z. we were informed that our soldier had shot himself in the knee to get out of the field. The implication being, take your time getting back to the hospital. I felt sorry for the guy, and gave him a cigarette and tried to make conversation with him. The trip must have been very painful for him. The question I have to ask is, "How much misery does it take before a guy shoots himself in the knee with an M-16 to escape it?"

The perimeter of our base camp was guarded by concertina wire and trip flares. There were also Claymore mines set out in case they come en-mass. One night after flying all day, I got back to find I had guard duty again. I had the "tower". It had a spotlight that we were supposed to shine every once in a while. We had radios so the captain of the guards could contact us if necessary. He would also walk from post-to-post occasionally to make sure the guy on guard duty wasn't asleep. So I had an idea. We were given an alarm that worked off a very fine copper wire. I decided to wrap the wire around the ladder. It would act as a last line of defense in case anybody tried to climb the ladder. It was a good plan, but it turned out to be unnecessary—it was a miserable night, and nobody came around. After this particular night I came down with some kind of illness that was like the flu. I felt terrible. I had to have someone walk over to sick call with me because I didn't know if I'd make it. I had a fever, but the Doc didn't know what was wrong. He may have given me some pills to take; I really don't remember. But I do remember waking up in the night soaking wet with sweat. In the morning I felt fine other than being exhausted.

I began to notice that I was getting guard duty almost every other day. This wasn't right. There were a lot more people to draw from than just me and one other poor slob. Finally I said something to one of my friends about all the guard duty I had been pulling. "That's easy," he said. "Don't you know what you're supposed to do?" He was surprised I had no clue. "This is what you do. When you see Sgt. Correia coming your way as your helicopter is landing, you jump out of the chopper and start yelling obscenities at him. Then start shaking your fist. I guarantee he will turn and go the other way."

So the next day as we came in for a landing, I spotted the Sarge coming my way. The helicopter was in the process of shutting down and the noise was considerable. I started shaking my fist and yelling, "Your ugly and your mother dresses you funny. And not only that, your grandma wears combat boots in the shower." Of course he couldn't hear a word I said with the noise of the helicopter shutting down. But if he did hear me, it was enough to make even the calmest guy mad. "What was that all about," asked the pilot. "A little experiment," I replied. The Sergeant turned and walked back the way he came. I never had guard duty again. It pays to be in the know.

The Tour

Pit Stop...

On a typical monsoon day, we were flying re-supply. Our pilot was trying to locate the encampment that needed to be re-supplied. It wasn't the first one of the day, as we had been re-supplying for hours. This particular spot seemed particularly difficult to locate. The clouds had descended to ground level, and we were running low on fuel. Base camp was too far away to go back. Our pilot called another ship from our Company. They had lots of fuel. He requested that they meet us at this particular encampment. We eventually found it. Flying low-level at a very slow rate of speed was a very dangerous procedure. We were vulnerable to being shot down. As we landed and got the helicopter shut down, the pilot tells me to transfer fuel from the other ship to ours. There was nothing to work with. The only way I was able to attempt this was to drain the fuel from a ¼ inch diameter drain on the belly of the helicopter. I found a small coffee can, and proceeded to lie on my back on the wet ground. I drained fuel into that small can, got up and walked over to our ship, and poured the fuel into the fuel fill opening. I repeated this process a million times (small exaggeration). I was not happy with the pilot for us being in this position. Keep in mind that fuel in our choppers was measured in hundreds of pounds.

Night Life...

Back at camp, big changes were going on. Foundations and slabs were being poured for our new living quarters. These quarters were to have 2x4 walls with wood siding up 6 feet, and screen on the top 2 feet.

The Tour

The screen was to let light and air in. We did have a few lights in the building for night use. There were a few individual rooms for the NCOs, with the rest of the building open.

Our Sergeant Correia occupied one such room. It was his misfortune to invoke the ire of a couple fellows who liked to smoke grass (not the football field stuff) in the early morning hours. These guys would sit outside Sgt Correia's window and sing "coo-coo-coo-Correia, Correia," for as long as it took to wake him up and get a reaction. The whole call sounded like some wild parrot in the jungle. They would then fade into the night. This continued night-after-night for weeks as the Sarge tried to find out who was responsible for this outrage. It wasn't long before the Sarge would be after these guys with rifle in hand; gun loaded and ready to shoot. I don't know who was really the winner of this little contest as coo-coo-Correia really did go cuckoo. They shipped him home for the duration. The other boys got heavier into drinking and grass. *We never did get our football grass!*

On the rebound...

To replace Sgt. Coo Coo, a Sgt. was brought in from the field. His name was Sgt. Grouliex. He was a French Canadian by birth, and had a slight accent. I found him to be quite pleasant most of the time, although he could also be quite annoying at times. He was a good sergeant, and I believe had the respect of the men. He had been wounded out in the field. A few months later, how that happened was told to me by one of our troops out in the jungle.

As we landed at a firebase, I noticed a soldier sitting on top of a bunker made of sand bags. We looked at each other for some time before he yelled over to me asking if I knew a particular Sergeant. I said, "Yes, he's my platoon sergeant." He asked, "Did he ever tell you how he got wounded?" I said, "No." He went on to explain, It seems they were in a firefight with the enemy one night, and apparently one of our troops bounced an M-79 (grenade) off a tree (it had to go at least 30 yards) and it exploded by him. The guy I talked to seemed rather pleased with that fact. I don't know how much of that went on, but I know it wasn't rare. Fortunately he survived the ordeal and seemed none the worse for it.

New Barracks…

One of the benefits of these new barracks was that we got lockers that we could hang clothes in and keep personal stuff in a neater and more accessible fashion. It was a touch that made life a little more comfortable. My sister, Carole, would send care packages that had stuff we couldn't get, like powdered milk. These things were kept in the locker until they were used up. Another thing she sent was "rum balls". Now these were chocolate candy with rum in them. By the time they got to me and the heat treatment they received, I'm willing to bet they were 100 proof. Those did not last long when word got out that I had some. I would at least get to taste one. Normally that was all it took. We would just sit and smile at each other.

One of the drawbacks of having these new barracks was that we had to fill sandbags to protect the barracks as soon as we got back from our daily flights. Normally, by the time we got back, we had already put in a 12 to 13-hour day, gone without lunch or dinner, and generally had a stressful day. Putting in an hour filling sandbags really chapped my hide. The Company already hired some locals to clean the barracks, why couldn't they hire them to fill sandbags during the day? Needless to say; we did it, and spent weeks and weeks doing it. It might have saved some lives later on, but we were exhausted from it.

Bathroom Lights…

One night the guy that bunked below me left the room to go to the toilet. I was in the top bunk reading as he left. Dennis was a short, good-looking kid with a good sense of humor. He was real easy to get along with and a good friend. The fact that he was maybe 5' 5" or 5' 6" never entered our conversation. I could imagine him, however, sitting there with his feet dangling and not touching the floor. As I was reading, I heard an awful scream. I looked out to see the bathroom lit up like Macy's at Christmas.(the bathroom had no lights). Then Dennis came running out with his pants around his ankles. Watching someone trying to run this way is hilarious in itself. This was a funny sight as I remembered that a few months before, Tom "The Bomb" had taken a trip flare and wrapped it with tape, pulled the pin, and thrown it in one of the pots. It must have taken months for the tape to come unwrapped. I don't know if it was the pot Dennis was sitting on or not, but it made for a hilarious sight to me.

One Shot…

Corporal Lee was a gunner for second platoon. He had been in the infantry, and then extended for a year to be a gunner on a Huey. Those in the field thought it was a glorious job. Unknown by most, he had married a Vietnamese girl and she was expecting a baby. He was working on getting her back to America. He was a quiet guy that said few words, and had been my gunner on a couple of occasions. It was hard to know what he was thinking. He was a very nice guy, in that he was polite and willing to do what was necessary to get the job done. He didn't, however, offer much conversation. When there was time to kill, conversation can be a plus.

The Second Platoon chopper was working re-supply and as they flew from one location to the next, flying low level, a shot rang out. The shot fired at a chopper flying 120 mph and passing a single location in the blink of an eye, hit Corporal Lee between the eyes and he was killed instantly. When the ship returned to base, Corporal Lee's body had been taken to Pleiku. The ship still had pieces of his skull that Jim Farrington and I got to wash out of his chopper.

Agent Orange...

Jim was a crew chief for Third Platoon (the one I was in). His chopper spent most of its time spraying Agent Orange around the countryside. This stuff was played down by the military as being safe, but Jim told me in no uncertain terms that that stuff was bad news. He showed me the sores and bumps that he had already started getting. It wasn't pretty. Of course using young kids for these types of missions was probably part of the plan. I always wondered, how much of that stuff got into our water?

The Tour

Capt. Gogo...

My friend Dennis (of trip flare fame) was crewing a ship that, while on a mission, lost power and crashed. As Dennis ran from the chopper covered in fuel, he tripped over a log and broke his leg. The crew was recovered, and they all survived the ordeal. One of the pilots on this mission was Captain Gogo. That wasn't his real name; but I could never pronounce (never mind spell) his real name. Let it suffice to say, he was of Polish decent. I was to have several memorable flights with Capt. Gogo in the time to come.

One such flight was a combat assault in which we were to drop off some Vietnamese troops into another location in the jungle. Normal procedure was to come in for a landing in the LZ, allow the troops to get out, tell the pilot we were clear; and at that point, we would take off. All this was done in a matter of seconds. However, that didn't happen this trip. As we came in for a landing and were about 15 feet off the ground, Capt. Gogo started screaming, "Get them out! Get them out!" He maintained a hover at that distance off the ground. We (the gunner and I) had no choice but to start telling these guys to get out. They got the message when we swung around the seat post and pointed to the ground. These guys were fully loaded with big backpacks, ammunition, and of course their rifles. The last guy out had the misfortune to land on a stump on his back. As he was leaving, I got back to my position on the M-60. He lay there for a second, and then pointed his rifle at us. I already had the M-60 pointed at him; so if he had any intentions of shooting at us, he changed his mind. Our chopper then departed, and I kept the M-60 on him until we were out of range.

The Tour

Cease Fire...

We were flying to an outpost location one glorious day. Flying low-level was the norm. Heading for the Cambodian border was not one of my favorite things. As we flew along, all of a sudden an explosion rocked the ship. An artillery shell exploded just off our right side. The pilot got on the radio and started yelling, "Cease fire! Cease fire!" Of course, at 100+ mph we cover a lot of ground in a short period of time. We had no more close encounters that flight. I still wonder what the trajectory of that shell was, and just how close it was. It certainly hit close to us.

Too Much Dust...

Every once in a while you hear a story that has more fiction than fact in it. Such is the case with the story about the chopper that came in for a landing at a firebase occupied by a tank outfit. It was during the dry season and the dust was awful. As the chopper began to land, of course the dust kicked up and the pilot was unable to see. As he sat there at a hover, he came down with vertigo, (losing his sense of up and down). He then asked the co-pilot to take over; and in the meantime, the dust continued to billow. The co-pilot eventually landed the chopper; they shut down, and trotted off to have their meeting with the firebase C.O. As the crew chief sat there he noticed something odd—a lump in the ground that he hadn't noticed before. He got out of the chopper, walked over to it, and kicked it with his boot. To his surprise, a steel pot (helmet) rolled away. As he looked down, his surprise turned to shock when he discovered a human head sticking out of the sand. As he stood there staring at the head, it began to speak, "Watch it pal, and don't just stand there. Get a shovel, the boys in this tank would like to get some lunch!"

New Guy...

Back at base camp, I finally had a day off. It was nice to de-stress. Capt. Files got a hold of me, and said he had a new pilot we needed to check out. We were going to use my ship. As we did the run-up, Capt Files asked the "New Guy" how he was with auto rotations—the art of shutting the motor down at say 500 feet above ground level, dropping to almost ground level, and suddenly pulling up on the collective stick to give a soft landing. "New guy" said he was good with them; so up we go. Capt Files gave him the controls and told him "cut power". He did, and down we came, closer and closer to the ground. I think "New Guy" pulled up on the collective after the first bounce. There were several more. Capt Files was not impressed, nor was I. "That needs a little work," was the understatement. "Can you fly a pattern?" Capt Files asked. "Sure I can do that," said New Guy. Off we went doing a typical pattern around the airfield. We got 100 feet off the ground: and while banking to the right, the chopper started vibrating severely. "New Guy" said he couldn't control it. Capt Files took over and called for an emergency landing. The vibration was intense. I was scanning the area to see if there was any sign of anything that we might have hit, like another aircraft or a bird, just anything. After we landed and the chopper was shut down, I started looking for what might have caused such a vibration.

The Tour

I checked the tubes that controlled the pitch on the rotor blades—they were fine. Everything I checked seemed okay. As I went to tie down the rotor blade, I found the problem—the cap at the end of the blade was missing. It probably weighed several pounds. The blades are balanced with little BBs at the rotor head. No wonder we had such a vibration. My chopper now had to go to maintenance for a new rotor blade. "New-Guy" made quite an impression.

What's this Button for...

A new aviation company was coming to town. The 173rd Airborne Aviation Company also wanted to make an impression. They did! On their first landing at our base, one of their choppers hit the wrong button and fired a rocket that hit one of our choppers. It, of course, blew up. However, these guys proved to be gutsy as they hovered above the trees and spread the branches so they could have a look. This proved to be a bad policy as several of them were shot down. They discontinued the practice.

Don't Shoot...

There were certain areas that, upon checking, we were certain had no "friendlies." This didn't seem to matter. Our fearless leaders came up with a policy that stated, "We were not to shoot unless shot at first." Our company commander was good at dodging grenades. Did he think we would be good at dodging bullets? It was like having a duel and telling the other guy, "You go ahead and shoot first." The difference being, these guys were using automatic weapons. We weren't happy about this change. Maybe they wanted us to throw rocks at them with notes tied to them saying, "We don't like you." Ahhh! So that's what all the rocks in the pockets was all about in basic training!

Love & War...

One of our gunners, who, on occasion, got himself into trouble, found out what real trouble was. He apparently found a girlfriend in Pleiku—not that she was the trouble. But because he decided to stay with her and forget about the Army and the war, the higher ups got upset. After all, where were his priorities? Make war, not love! So they sent the local police to check on him. That's when his troubles really started. An argument ensued, and our gunner pulled a gun and shot the police officer. As far as I know he's still there. What I want to know is; where did he get the gun? All our handguns were taken away some time ago. And bullets, how does a guy (a little on the unstable side) get bullets, when us crew chiefs couldn't even have a gun?

The Race...

On one flight, the pilots decided we should test our machine guns. We were near the Pleiku airfield on our way to our final destination. As we were going past, I noticed a Vietnamese A-1 Skyraider aircraft coming in for a landing. As he touched down, the napalm bomb he was carrying, let go. It hit the runway and exploded and it followed the plane down the runway. We heard the Vietnamese tower talking to the pilot as they frantically told him to abort his landing and put the pedal to the metal. It took him a little time to get the drift of what was happening, and the napalm seemed to be catching up. He finally got more speed, and outran his pursuing cargo. I'm sure it was a tremendous relief for him and the tower.

When we did finally get to test fire our weapons, the result was not a confidence builder. As I fired the M-60, it fired one shot then jammed. "Try your rifle," was the pilot's suggestion. I grabbed my M-16, and pulled the trigger. One shot rang out, and then it jammed. I was really hoping we weren't going to run into the enemy. The M-16 was notorious for jamming once it had a little dust on it. The M-60 was normally extremely dependable. Our gunner was embarrassed by the machine gun not firing, and he made sure to clean the guns as soon as we landed. We never again had trouble with the machine guns.

Hot Pursuit...

One of our many missions was either picking up or inserting Long Range Reconnaissance Patrols (LRRPs). Normally it was no problem doing either. On this one occasion, picking the LRRPs up caused some excitement. We were called to pick them up at a given location. The next call we received was an urgent call that they were being chased, and the enemy was in hot pursuit. These guys had come upon a series of bunkers with weapons and an assortment of other gear. Apparently the enemy wasn't home at the time. They came home. This wartime game of "The Three Bears" got real serious in a hurry. The LRRPs were running as fast as they could with a captured .50 cal. machine gun. It was a big gun to carry while running for your life. They also had an AK-47 (the Russian-made automatic rifle). The LZ was changed because these guys didn't think they could make it to the original one and live.

We dropped into a spot that was on the way to the original location. It was only a few minutes before these guys came running up and jumping into the chopper. As the last one got in, we opened fire with our machine guns, and the pilots lifted off. The fellow with the stolen Chinese machine gun was kissing the floor of the chopper as we flew off. Obviously he was extremely happy to be saved from an untimely death. I believe our cover fire kept the enemy from firing on us. We were out of the area in short order.

Smoke...

Combat assaults were also a regular part of our schedule. It involved picking up the troops at one location and dropping them at another. Typically, the second location was not secure. That meant as we dropped the troops in, we would lay down cover fire at the tree line with our M-60 machine guns. One such combat assault got off to a bad start through no fault of our own. Flying in formation was a typical combat assault (C/A) procedure. Normally there was a lead ship, with one ship behind to the right and one to the left. In effect, a "V." To help identify their location, the troops on the ground throw a colored smoke grenade. Upon visual sighting of the smoke, the aircrew confirms the color with the ground troops. This procedure helps prevent the enemy from throwing a smoke grenade and luring us to the wrong location.

One July day as the lead ship (us) identified white smoke, we received acknowledgement that the location, indeed, did have white smoke. We dropped in, and came in for a landing. The other two ships were right behind us. As our rotor blades caught the white smoke and it wafted into our helicopter we realized that smoke wasn't smoke, but C.S. gas (tear gas). The pilot immediately radioed to the other aircraft, "Abort! Abort!" All three ships left at the same time. I don't know how the pilots could see—my eyes were burning for some time after. Needless to say, some joker threw out tear gas instead of white smoke. I doubt if he made the sergeant's list—except maybe the list that involved a lot of stirring.

Wild Things...

Every once in a while in life, we may get to witness something very few people have ever seen. Such was the case one trip, flying low-level on our way to Dak To. As we came to a clearing, my eyes were fixed on the tree line. With machine gun at the ready, at the tree line were two Bengal tigers laying at the edge of the clearing. I asked the pilot if he saw them. He said he didn't, and turned the ship around to have a look; but by then, they were gone.

The Tour

CHAPTER
18

The New "H" Model...

Shortly after the end of the monsoon season, we got a new chopper to replace the aging "D" models. The new models were "H" models. The difference between 1300hp versus 1100hp was huge. We no longer worried about losing power in the mountains.

On one of the first fights with our new chopper, we were flying re-supply in an area that we didn't normally fly. It was in the afternoon, and we were looking forward to getting back to our camp. Of course we were flying low-level, and there were times it got very monotonous—this was one of those times. We apparently passed by a clearing that I did not see. The A/C said to me, "Chief did you see that?" "What?" I replied. He said, "Those troops in that clearing." I replied sheepishly; "No." "Well we're going to go have another look." So he turned that chopper around, made a big circle, and came past going the same direction. This time we were going a little slower. I was shocked at what I saw.

There were between 50 and 75 troops out in the open. They froze and did not move while we were looking at them. The pilot got on the radio and started checking to see if we had any "Friendlies" in the area. The answer was "No." The problem was that it took so long to find out if they were friendlies or not; we were already out of the area. Also, I wasn't clear on our policy of, "Waiting to get shot at first." Whether they ALL had to shoot first, and THEN we could fire; or if we just had to wait for a FEW to shoot. I'm glad we didn't find out, because if there was a shoot-out, they had a lot better odds.

Bullets Flying...

On occasion we would go "out of town" and stay at another base for several days. On such occasions we would usually fly a re-supply mission; and in the process, pick up troops that are either wounded or due for rotation. On one of these trips, we had just picked up two soldiers and were heading to our next location at about 200 feet above the ground. Our pilot was trying to get a fix on the next location when we started receiving fire from automatic weapons. One shot hit the ship. I couldn't fire because we were so close to our own troops. Our ground troops told our pilot to be quiet on the radio because they heard shooting. His reply, "Yeah, they're shooting at us." I saw the one infantry troop closest to me flinch. We were in a bad spot. That altitude made us sitting ducks. The pilot nosed it down and we started losing altitude. When all was said and done, we found the initial bullet went through the pilots' door, ricocheted off the armor plating, and headed straight for me. The jump seat happened to be in the "up" position. This may have saved my life. The bullet went through the 1/2-inch wide seat post and then through the nylon seat bottom and fell into the fold of the seat. Crew chiefs and gunners normally sat on one half of a bulletproof vest and wear another. These vests covered front and back, but not our sides. That is where that bullet was headed. It stopped 6 inches from me. Metal fragments hit the infantry guy closest to me and stuck in his arm. When we got on the ground he was sure to show me. I don't think he was going to volunteer to be a gunner. Oh well! We couldn't convince them all.

That would have been even harder once I found out that we took several rounds that day. This particular flight was the first mission I flew with "new guy" since the test flight where he broke my helicopter. And it turned out to be his last. After this flight, he quit flying and took a desk job. I don't imagine the Army was too happy with him after investing all that time and money to make him a pilot.

Night Duty...

Once in a while, each flight team had night duty. We were either on flare duty or regular night duty. Flare duty, to me, was the most dangerous mission one could fly. The pilots were not in danger, just me. The helicopter was stocked with parachute flares. These flares were about 3 inches in diameter; about 2 feet long, and were stacked on both sides of the ship. They were stacked in a pyramid about 30 inches high, and had a cable that was attached to a ring in the floor. What made this dangerous was that both doors were open, there was no place to sit, and there was no equipment or device to keep the crew chief from falling out. Not to mention the fact it was nighttime, and there is no horizon to know how much lean the chopper was in. In addition to all this, the flares had to clear the skids when I kicked them out or they could ignite beside the fuel tank. All this is to say nothing of what the enemy could do if they got a glimpse of our location. Luckily this was not a job I had very often.

One night duty mission we had was to fly a General back to Pleiku. It wasn't a long flight, and the pilots flew fairly high. On the way back, I noticed a basketball on fire heading up at us. Apparently it wasn't a basketball but a .50-caliber tracer round one of the fine folks of Pleiku decided to send our way. Perhaps they were trying to light our way; and if so, it was mighty neighborly.

The Tour

POW...

Back in the daylight hours, we received a call to go pick up a POW. He was a North Vietnamese that had been captured in a shootout with U.S. troops. As we landed to pick him up, the first thing I noticed was a stack of human bodies. They were all North Vietnamese stacked like cordwood. It was not a pretty site. The POW had been shot. He was loaded in the chopper, and we flew him to Pleiku Hospital. On the flight as I watched him, he was obviously very scared and in shock from being shot and from losing his friends. I thought I heard sometime later that he survived. The age of those troops did not seem to differ much from that of our own. Young men pushed into war, not knowing how cruel and harsh it can be.

Goodbye Rocks...

Back at camp we wanted to rest up, but the Army had different plans. It seems the Commanding General was leaving, so the brass wanted a parade. I don't like parades. Besides, I didn't have any rocks for my pocket, and there wasn't time to get any. I tried using that excuse, but of course they weren't buying it. So, march we did. Of the many things that seem stupid to me, marching around in dress uniform in a war zone is right up there near the top. It didn't seem to make a bit of difference that we were getting a new general, just as it didn't make much difference if we got a new troop in. The war went on the same. The food was still the same. And all the BS we had to put up with was the same. We didn't see the new guy, just like we didn't see the old guy.

The Tour

The 3rd platoon of the 4th Aviation Battalion, 4th Infantry Division (us), on a regular basis supported the 3rd Battalion, 12th Infantry of the 4th Infantry Division. We called them 3rd of the 12th. Mid-summer they were close to the Cambodian border when they were attacked. They were outnumbered severely, and overrun. Most of the company was killed. During the attack, they refused help from our choppers. The reason: "It was too dangerous for us." What bravery! The time it took for air strikes to occur would have been too late. After it was over, Dennis and T.J., his gunner, went to pick up bodies. Dennis was initially unable to help. He stood there looking at the carnage. It seemed to shock him so bad that all he could do was look. That moment changed him from then on.

My ship flew out there the next day with the Battalion Commander looking for any sign of the enemy. The enemy's procedure was to move across the border, engage U.S. forces and run back across the border. Of course, we aren't allowed across the border. We flew right on the border at tree top level. On one occasion, the pilot banked so hard that our rotor blades hit the treetops. It sounded like a rifle shot, which raised everyone's heart rates. We didn't find anything. That was no surprise either.

The Tour

Bob Hope…

One of the things that every troop in a war zone looks forward to is a visit from Bob Hope. Our base was no exception. I have no idea how long it took to prepare for his visit, but I knew nothing about it until the last minute. Of course when you are out flying all the time, most information passes you by. The show was held at our base, and the location was a big bowl of sorts. The show was packed, with the majority sitting on the ground on the hillside. So by the time I get to the show, the only place to sit is up on top of a hill that overlooks the stage. Bob looked like an ant. When he would crack a joke, guys up front would laugh and we'd be saying, "What did he say?" This went on for some time until finally I'd had enough and left. I guess it was a good show. There were so many guys there that I had to wonder; who was minding the war.

Faux Pas…

I haven't mentioned any real faux pas that our pilots might have committed. I only know of two. The first one was a trip up the river with a couple of "doughnut dollies." These girls were American, and probably were the first the pilots had seen in 8 months. So boys being boys, they were hot-dogging along the river when a rotor blade caught the river; and at that point; it was all over. No one was killed, but a doughnut dolly got a broken arm. The helicopter was destroyed. As far as I know, they were never able to find it. It was miraculous that no one was killed.

The second incident was a simple thing. Our chopper was slinging (carrying with net and sling) a 1-ton load of C-4 plastic explosive. As they were flying along talking, someone hit the wrong button and dropped the load. Not a big deal, right? Wrong! They were never able to find it. I'm sure the enemy would be happy to find it.

During one of our firebase "oasis" outings, we were sitting waiting for an assignment. We heard an explosion just behind the perimeter, and got the call shortly thereafter. In minutes, we were in the air. In about 10 seconds we were at the location. The enemy used a rocket-propelled grenade, and hit an armored personnel carrier. One man was seriously wounded, and was carried in a poncho (raincoat) to the ship. In seconds we were back to the "oasis." However, I believe the soldier died while in the helicopter. The enemy slipped away into a nearby village and was never caught.

The Deception…

The enemy used many tactics to overcome their lack of mobility (in comparison to ours), and the fact they were outgunned. One of the tactics was to set a trap of having a man lie in the open to lure a helicopter crew in. The tree line was full of enemy troops waiting to open fire. This occurred with our Company Commander (Major) and the Battalion Commander (Lt. Colonel). I don't know if they were told about the man lying beside the log, or if they saw him. They did, however, go into the clearing carrying an infantry Captain who was trying to oversee his troops in the field. As they entered for a landing, the tree line erupted with enemy fire killing the infantry Captain. My friend Steve, the crew chief, opened fire with his M-60 machine gun. They did not capture the enemy, and my friend Steve was shot. They flew back to Pleiku to the hospital but it was too late for the Captain. As they unloaded him, Steve asked the Major, "Should I get off too?" "Why?" asked the major, "Are you hit?" "Yes Sir," was Steve's reply. So off he went. His injuries were not life threatening, and he returned to us some time later. An interesting side note to this is that the Major put the Colonel in for a "Distinguished Flying Cross," and the Colonel did the same for the Major. They both received them.

Please don't get me wrong; there were thousands of brave acts done by pilots in Vietnam. Some were noticed; most were not. It was an everyday (brave) thing just doing what they did.

Weekend Away…

Every once in awhile, we got a chance to get away from the craziness for a day or two. Our escape was to fly down to the Saigon area to pick up gunship armament. The A/C (aircraft commander) (the guy that lost his skids and ran us out of fuel) and I argued about whether we were going to be armed. I wanted us to take the M-60's; he did not. His argument was that we would be flying at high altitude and wouldn't need them. He also did not want the extra weight. "What about take off and landings?" I argued. "What if our mission changes while we are there?" I added. "I'm pulling rank" he said. "We are not taking the guns!" So off we went. One of the very few times while flying in Vietnam that I got to fly with the doors closed. No worries. The trip there was very uneventful. While coming in for a landing and flying over a bunch of rice paddies, I felt naked. Many of those working in the rice paddies looked at us and studied the ship. No doubt they didn't see one without guns very often. I kept my eye on as many as I could. Not that I could do anything if they started to shoot. *Where were my rocks anyway?* We got our load of rocket pods and other miscellaneous armament. It was getting toward evening. We spent the night there and took off in the morning.

The trip back followed the coast. We got to Cam Ranh Bay and headed inland. We were about an hour out of Cam Ranh Bay and in the mountains when the A/C yelled out that we had "lost transmission oil pressure." Now I must explain that helicopters can lose engines, fuel, and miscellaneous parts, and still land safely. If it loses its transmission, you have a rock with doors. "Chief what do we do?" was the A/C's question. I had to think. Finally I asked him to watch the EGT (exhaust gas temperature). If it goes up, that means the engine is working harder to turn the rotors. "Mayday, Mayday," was the A/C's call. "This is Blackjack 613. We have lost transmission oil pressure". Another ship answered back, "What is your location?" This went on for a while until our pilot asked, "where was the closest U.S. base." We got a fix on that location, and headed towards it. I figured, "Oh great, we're going down and we have no guns, if we even survive". If you lose the transmission at low level, you might have a chance; at 5,000 feet, there is no chance. We continued to fly to the U.S. base. There were no new noises or other signs (i.e. gauges etc.). We finally landed after a 45-minute detour. The maintenance crew at the base changed the gauge and off we went none the worse for wear. We arrived back at our base late in the evening. The mess hall was closed—lucky for us.

Hill 875…

Hill 875 was one of those strategic places in the Dak To area that we abandoned in the monsoon season due to an inability to re-supply the troops there. When we did so, the enemy would take the hill. When the monsoons were over, we would try to retake it. It was a bad place—it cost many lives capturing and trying to retain the hill.

The 173rd Airborne were charged with recapturing the hill. The enemy was well dug in by the time the weather cleared. After days of fighting the 173rd finally got to the top, but the cost of American lives was way too high. The next night they were attacked and almost overrun. They called in an air strike on their own position. Many men were killed when the napalm hit the top of that hill. Some were the enemy; some were ours.

The next day we flew onto that hill. It was very steep, so they made us an 8-foot-square landing pad of logs. The pilots shut the chopper down, and we walked around looking at the carnage. While we were on the hill, there was a noise in the area of the chopper. As we looked, we noticed the logs supporting the chopper were starting to roll down the hill. The chopper pitched backwards and sat on its tail boom. It was very precarious. We ran for the chopper. The pilots jumped in and started it up. For a moment it looked as if the chopper could roll down the hill and be destroyed. The pilots brought the helicopter to a hover, and the gunner and I were able to jump on. Off we went to the airfield at Dak To.

From there, our mission was to take American bodies back to Pleiku. They were in body bags lined up next to each other. There were many. We carried them (as many as we could) to our ship and loaded them in. We then flew to Pleiku. It was a very somber flight.

The Tour

Mortars...

Our next flight to Dak To was a day later. We shut down on the side of the runway on the west end. It was only a few minutes before the mortars started dropping in. They started on the north side of the airfield at the east end of the runway. On the south side were four C-130 aircraft unloading artillery shells. The gunner and I ran towards the east end of the runway to investigate. The mortars kept coming. One aircraft was hit and was leaking fuel. One brave soul grabbed an aircraft tug and started pulling the C-130s away. We were about 50 yards from the closest aircraft. Mortars had hit the artillery shell storage area just beyond the planes. Rounds were going off. A piece landed by us, along with darts from a beehive round. One C-130 was able to take off; another was in the process. The mortars and artillery shells that were going off were  destroying the other two. We decided that maybe we should get back to our helicopter. By this time, helicopter gun ships were blasting the hills with rockets. Later, jets and other World War II planes would take part in blasting the hillsides that the enemy was dug into. We left after the hillside started getting blasted. The artillery storage area exploded into the next day.

The Tour

Leopard Skin Leotards...

Our next mission to Dak To was a snoopy mission—you remember the machine that picked up smoke and ammonia scents? We flew treetop-level as usual. In these mountains it was not easy. The pilots became very proficient at negotiating the mountains. We had flown this mission many times. As we crested the top of one mountain, the chopper wanted to just keep going into space. That would have made us real easy targets because our air speed was so low by the time we got to the top. So the pilot would drop the collective, give the chopper some hard right or left pedal, and we would side slip down the mountain. The affect to me was that as soon as he dropped the collective, I would come out of my sitting position and immediately be standing. I did not want to be standing. It is too easy to fall out of the aircraft when you are standing. So I would sit down only to have the same thing happen at the next mountaintop.

We were picking up smells quite frequently. We finally were flying level and in a valley. I heard something hit the ship. As I looked ahead, I saw two men kneeling down and firing at us. They were in the open on the side of a hill. It appeared they were using AK-47 automatic rifles. I returned fire with the M-60. As we passed, they threw down their rifles and started to run for the tree line above them, I stood out on the gun mount, still firing. I was glad there was a stop on the gun mount because I probably would have shot the tail boom. Also, as we passed these guys our engine chip detector warning light came on. (This detected metal particles in the engine.) This concerned the pilot. He radioed in our situation, and also that we had been fired on. The infantry guy on the ground we were flying the mission for, asked what they were wearing. *I was tempted to tell him leopard skin leotards with purple polka dot shirts.* When all was said and done, the infantry guy said "We thought they were there."

As it turns out a bullet had been a foot low from hitting me— and these jokers <u>thought</u> they were there! Man, that really chaps my hide. I don't mind people going fishing as long as I'm not the bait! The day this happened, I had 19 days left in that country.

Thanksgiving...

We received a very unexpected surprise at Thanksgiving. It turned out that the new commanding General was coming to dinner. As guys who flew everyday and arriving back at base long after the mess hall closed, we knew nothing about it. Of course the very finest food and accessories were prepared and we were actually able to partake of the meal. The only problem was that we ate so little for months on end that our eyes were definitely bigger than our stomachs. Just the fact that we could drink out of glasses, instead of bowls, was quite a treat.

Christmas...

Christmas was a special day for the crew of our ship. We had our chopper fitted with a giant loudspeaker and we flew for hours over the jungle trying to talk the NVA into turning themselves in and becoming our friends. I doubt it did any good as the sound seemed to be garbled and very hard to understand. Of course it was in Vietnamese which I did not speak.

Mortars Galore…

It was normal procedure that when a guy got down to one week left in-country, he would be taken out of the field and just work on processing out. I wanted to get to that point. With two weeks left in-country, I suggested to our captain that since flying was voluntary, I would like to go back to maintenance for my last week. He offered to take this to the Company Commander, which he did. In the meantime, we had another mission in Dak To. As we flew re-supply across the valley, we were at a dangerous altitude. We started to drop down when mortars started exploding in front of us. It wasn't as though there was one over here, and one over there. They were everywhere. We hit the deck and hoped for the best. There were 10 to 15 on each side of us going off at any one time. I don't know how this was even possible. Was it the enemy who saw us coming, and decided to open up? We didn't know. As the pilot got on the radio and shouted, "Cease fire" on every frequency he could, a mortar went off right beside our ship. It rocked us over; but no one was hit, and we continued through the barrage. It seemed like forever. How we made it through that, I do not know. Truly the Lord had to be looking out for us. Even as I think about it today, it seems impossible that we made it through safely.

Back at camp I got an answer to my request. The CO said that if I didn't fly, I would be court-martialed. I didn't care. If they wanted to take my rank and the medals I was to receive, that didn't matter. They could keep those. I didn't want to give them my life though. We settled on a compromise thanks to Captain Files. I ended up flying some easy missions, and survived the duration.

The Tour

CHAPTER

19

Going Home...

The processing out part of all this, left a sour taste in my mouth as I knew the Company Commander wanted to court-martial me. I did not have a high opinion of him anyway. Not that he or anyone else cared what I thought. Regardless of what he thought of me, there was one thing he could not deny—I survived! No matter what they sent me to do, no matter what the odds; I survived! I know they sent me to do things they didn't send anyone else to do. I know they did not like me. None of that matters; because in the end, I did what they asked and I survived! I honestly believe that my survival was not from anything that I did; but rather, the work of my Lord and Savior, Jesus Christ. He knew what my future was to hold. He also knew that I did not deserve to be saved. Not then, not now, and not in the future. His love, however, is never ending, never changing, and always there. All we have to do is accept it! It took me many more years before I realized He was there, and He knew that! He saved me anyway.

Our trip home started in a CH47 Chinook helicopter. We flew to Pleiku, and from there we caught a C-123 cargo plane to Cam Ranh Bay. We spent the night there, and waited all day for our flight on a commercial jet. I don't remember much about the flight other than we landed in Tokyo for a couple hours. I stayed in the airport. Leaving seemed surreal. It was something we all wanted for that one year, and finally it was happening. From what I recall, the flight was 21 to 23 hours. We arrived in Seattle on a cold January night. We took a taxi to a hotel for the night. Upon checking in, the hotel clerk asked, "Kill any babies?" My blood started to boil, but I let it go. We just wanted to get home. The next morning I flew to San Francisco and was met there by my parents. It was great to be home again. The folks had a nice banner up welcoming me home. It was a great end to my overseas duty.

Home at Last…

We all received a 30-day leave upon arriving back home. During this time, Mom and Dad and I traveled up to B.C. where we visited with Aunt Daisy, Uncle Bert, and Richard. On the way up, I called my friend Dennis to plan a visit with him and have my folks meet him. Dennis lived in the Seattle area. We had a good visit, and Dennis asked where we were going. I told him we were going up to B.C., and asked if he wanted to go. He said if he could take his car he would love to go. It was decided that Dennis and I would go together, and Mom and Dad would proceed by themselves. The folks left while Dennis was getting his stuff packed up. I must explain that Dennis had ordered a new car while we were in Vietnam. He was so happy with it that I guess he just couldn't stand to leave it at home. It was a 1968 Plymouth GTX. Those cars came standard with a 440 cubic-inch motor that would get up and scoot. It was a really nice looking car that was sure to impress the girls, we thought. As we came into my old hometown of Haney, we cruised on into the local A&W. We did order something, but really we were looking for girls. It was a cool January night and very few patrons were in the establishment. We soon left and found ourselves at a stoplight waiting for it to change. A car pulled up beside us, and to our amazement, there were two girls in the car. We tried not to look overly interested, but we had just come from Vietnam where we saw no girls for a year! As we sat there hoping to at least get a glance, they both stared straight ahead. It seemed like we waited 20 minutes for some sort of look— nothing.

When the light changed Dennis did something that surprised me. He jumped on the gas, and for a second that car just sat there and smoked the tires. It soon started fishtailing through the intersection. I looked to my right and coming the other way was a local Royal Canadian Mounted Police. Not riding a horse, or wearing a red jacket and driving a team of dogs, but driving a patrol car. I yelled at Dennis, "Shut it down, there's a cop!" He drove a short distance to the next street and turned right and then pulled over. "What are you doing?" I asked. "The cop was right behind me so I pulled over,;" he said. It was dark and hard to tell who was behind us. The car that Dennis thought was the cop went past us and to our surprise, it was not the cop. "I'm getting out of here," Dennis said as he pulled away from the curb. Just as he pulled away from the curb, the patrol car came around the corner. The chase was on. Dennis sped to the next corner and turned right. He sped down that street, and turned right again. Now we are going the same direction on the same street I first saw the Mountie. We flew through the intersection; luckily the light was green—we didn't want to break any traffic laws. We came to River Road, which as the name implies, goes along the river. We turned left onto that road, and Dennis put his foot into it. It was a gravel road that we were speeding down at 90mph. There were three Indians coming up the riverbank; and as we passed, they jumped back down the bank. The Mountie was ¼-mile behind us with his lights on and in hot pursuit.

The highway out of town was coming up, and we wasted no time getting on it. As we flew along, I asked Dennis, "How fast are we going?" He replied, "130." I told Dennis to take the next left. He did that, and we were instantly going up a street that had no lighting. This road was like a roller coaster, and Dennis was having a hard time with it. We were doing about 90mph when Dennis tells me, "I can't control it." I instantly had a flashback to Vietnam when the pilot yelled out those very words. "What do you mean you can't control it?" I asked. He repeated his statement this time with irritation in his voice. I had no idea what sort of problem he was talking about; but decided we needed to get off this road we were on, so we could find out. We didn't know if the Mountie was still on our tail or not. "Dennis, take a right," I said. He did and we were now on a road I really didn't remember. As we poked along, I saw a driveway that went down a small hill. "Go left into that driveway," I said. As we got down to the bottom of the hill, we got out to survey the problem. We were in some sort of a commercial-type yard that had no lighting and no apparent buildings. What our problem turned out to be was a flat tire. No problem, we would just change the tire and be on our way before the police showed up. Dennis went to the trunk, pulled out his lug wrench and jack, then went to the front of the car. He tried each of the four sockets on the lug wrench, and none of them fit his mag wheel nuts.

Now we had a real problem. Not that being fugitives from the law wasn't a problem; but we now had no way to escape this situation. It wasn't long before we heard a vehicle coming up the road the way we came. It seemed to slow down when it got closer to us. The gravity of our situation did not escape either of us. We had been back home for a week and now we were fugitives from the law of another country, and we might be going to jail. The Army policy seemed to be that once the civilian law got through with you, the military law would then exact its punishment. If we had much time in jail, we would then be AWOL (absent without leave), which the Army seemed to frown on.

As we walked to the trunk of the car, I said to Dennis, "We're in for it now!" The car that had been coming our way pulled up to the top of the driveway and shined a spotlight down on us. "We are done for," I said. The car stayed in the same spot for what seemed like an eternity. "He's calling for backup," I said. After what had to be at least five minutes, the person in the vehicle yelled down to us, "What are you doing?" That was an odd question coming from a police officer. Our answer was, "We're trying to change a tire." There was a short pause, and then the vehicle slowly pulled down beside Dennis's car. It then became obvious that the vehicle was not a cop car at all. The driver got out and asked, "What seems to be the problem?" We explained to him that the lug wrench didn't fit. He opened up his trunk and pulled out some sockets, found one that fit, and proceeded to help us change the tire. He explained that we had pulled down into a gravel pit and lately they had some thievery going on. So they had the area wired for sound; and when we pulled down in there, it set off an alarm. It was his job to check it out. We thanked him for his help, and went on our way. We went 30 miles out of our way to avoid my good old home town from then on.

After a short visit with Uncle Bert, Aunt Daisy, and Cousin Richard, we headed over to Piers Island. It is a little island off Vancouver Island in British Columbia . I wanted to go look at the lot I purchased while I was stationed in Washington. It was still there, and looked the same as I remembered. The picture taken from this lot at sunset was something that helped me get through all the things that happened. It was in my locker and I looked at it every day.

The Tour

CHAPTER 20

Fort Knox...

All too soon my leave was over, and I needed to start out for my next assignment—Fort Knox, Kentucky. I decided to drive there for want of transportation once I was there. The trip was mostly uneventful other than sleeping over night in the back seat of the car behind a gas station in Albuquerque, New Mexico. I had a very light sleeping bag (that you could see through), and it got very cold that early March night. I woke in the early morning hours to find a half-inch of ice on the windshield (on the inside of the car). That took a while to clean up. When it got light, I drove a few miles to the ski resort that gave an excellent view of the city. I was soon off, driving through the Texas panhandle and into Oklahoma, across that fine state, and up into Missouri. I drove across Missouri, the lower part of Illinois and Indiana, and into Louisville, Kentucky. From there, Hwy.31W took me to Ft. Knox. It was a long trip and I worried about running out of money before getting there. Therefore, I spent several nights sleeping in the back of the car—you can do that when you are young.

Ft. Knox was an interesting place, and home of the US Army Armor Center. Armor, meaning tanks and APCs. The area had rolling hills and oak trees, and many other types of big leafed trees. Those trees at this point, however, had no leaves. In the springtime, it was a pretty place. The big question I had been asking myself was, "What are they going to have us do?" There did not seem to be any helicopters here to work on. We were booked (I mean, assigned) into a sort of holding company, much like that of Ft. Lewis; the difference being this company assigned duties daily, unless you volunteered for some assignment. For example, they wanted some men to test out some rafts on the Ohio River. This didn't sound like fun to me because it was still winter. I later tried out for a lifeguard position that would be at one of the on-base pools. This I figured would take place when the weather got warmer. It turned out to be a great job. The first sergeant didn't like it because he didn't get to keep an eye on us. One of the other lifeguards and I rented an apartment off post, and we lived the high life. It was like we were not in the Army, which was great. I had a second and third job that helped to pay for this extravagance. The second job was working at a gas station from 11:00pm to 8:00am on Friday nights. The third job started Saturday morning. I worked for a trash disposal company from 8:00am to whenever we finished, which was normally around 2:00pm. I didn't go looking for that job as they came to me at the gas station and begged me to work. It seems their man scheduled for that shift was permanently missing. It made for a long night, and I was plenty tired by the time I got off.

The job of being a lifeguard was normally very uninteresting. On the day the under-privileged kids came from Louisville, things got more exciting. It was a challenging job to watch all those kids at one time. One particular hot summer day, I was watching as a young man was going under. He came back up flailing his arms, then went back down again. He was about ten feet from the side of the pool, and went down for a third time. It was time to act. I blew the whistle and dove into the pool after him. I retrieved him, pulled him up, carried him to the side of the pool, and set him on the edge. At that point he stated, "Put me down fool. What do you think you're doing?" His friends were laughing at him, and he was mad. It just goes to show you can't please some people even if you save their life.

On April 4, of 1968 Martin Luther King was assassinated in Memphis. As the summer heated up, there was rioting in cities all across the US. We were called to come back to our units and start riot training. The training went on for weeks, and we were finally assigned to go to Detroit. We were on high alert and not allowed off the base. We were scheduled on a flight, and all our gear was packed. At the last minute, the flight was cancelled. Why, I don't know. We were ordered to stand down, (which meant to go back to our regular duties). By this time, I was getting ready to process out early to go back to Chabot College.

Payday came around, and I needed to report to my company to get paid. That particular day I was feeling rather tipsy from the night before. As I walked along towards our company office, I spotted a flower growing in amongst a bunch of weeds. I thought, "Wouldn't that make me look snappy." So I picked it and put it in my lapel. Normally when we reported for pay we were in uniform, but I was practicing to be a civilian. When I stepped in the office and reported for pay, you'd have thought I just committed murder. The First Sergeant came unglued and got very red in the face. At that point I wondered, "Do I know this guy from somewhere?" He reminded me of that sergeant on the boat when we arrived in Vietnam. Maybe that's why he didn't like me! I was forced to take the flower out, and then had to report to the pay officer. "Specialist Bain reporting for pay, sir." I said. "What the hell…Oh well, here's your pay," was the pay officer's reply as he shook his head and mumbled something under his breath. I'm guessing that I didn't look as snappy as I thought. Of course, I didn't have the flower.

Within a couple of weeks, I needed to process out. That meant going back to that First Sergeant to have him sign my checklist. So to prepare, I got a haircut. As I reported to him, he eyed me up and down and said, "You need a haircut." But I just came from there, First Sergeant," I said. "I don't give a damn where you came from," he said. "Yes, First Sergeant," I said, eating a giant sized crow. So back I went to the barbershop. "Sarge said it wasn't good enough," I said. He stood there and I could read his mind, "Why don't you just go along with these guys, Dumbass?" He did cut on my hair one more time, although not much came off. This time, the Sarge signed off on my paperwork; and I was officially out of the Army. At no time in my military career did they ask me to re-up. Why is dat??

POSTSCRIPT

The stories of our Company and its men are just those I could remember; most are what I experienced. If you talked to someone else in my platoon, you would get a whole different set of experiences.

All of us are here by the grace of God and there is no other way to put it. I thank God that he has allowed me to get to this point in my life, even though Vietnam was not the only life-threatening situation I would have. For some people, it takes a long time to get the message; others never get the message. I will write about my other life-threatening situations later. None were the magnitude of Vietnam, but close calls just the same.

Within a month after we got home, our base was mortared and several crewmembers were killed and others wounded. I hope they let the guys have their guns back at night. I can't think of anything worse than being attacked at night, and not having a weapon to fight with.

The Tour

STATISTICS

The following statistics were taken from The National Vietnam Veterans Foundation, Inc.

- 9,087,000 military personnel served on active duty during the Vietnam Era (August 5, 1964 - May 7, 1975).
- 2,709,918 Americans served in Vietnam, this number represents 9.7% of their generation.
- Total Deaths: 58,202 (Includes men formerly classified as MIA and Mayaguez casualties). Men who have subsequently died of wounds account for the changing total.
- 61% of the men killed were 21 or younger.
- Wounded: 303,704 -- 153,329 hospitalized + 150,375 injured requiring no hospital care.
- Missing in Action: 2,338
- POWs: 766 (114 died in captivity)
- As of January 15, 2004, there are 1,875 Americans still unaccounted for from the Vietnam War.

LINKS

If you're interested in additional information about the Vietnam War, specific battles,

- The Battle of Dak To:
  http://en.wikipedia.org/wiki/Battle_of_dak_to

- The National Vietnam Veterans Foundation
  http://nationalvietnamveteransfoundation.org/

- Ernie Camacho, Air Traffic Controller, Dak To, 1967
  http://twirlonup.com/dakto/

- My Old Unit (4th Infantry Division, 4th Aviation Battalion)
  http://www.armyflightschool.org/vietnam/index.html

The Tour

Larry Bain lives in the foothills of Northern California with his wife of 43 years and his many horses.

To contact Larry email carpenterlarryb@gmail.com.

Made in the USA
Las Vegas, NV
27 January 2023

66317614R00074